JEWELRY FOR GENTLEMEN

JEWELRY FOR GENTLEMEN

JAMES SHERWOOD

SPECIAL PHOTOGRAPHY BY
ANDY BARNHAM

WITH 275 ILLUSTRATIONS

'For the London Leopards: Solange Azagury-Partridge,
Shaun Leane, Susan Farmer, Theo Fennell, Stephen Webster
and Carol Woolton, who inspired and encouraged
Jewelry for Gentlemen.'

Half-title page. Lizard lapel
pin (c.1860s) from Bentley
& Skinner set with graduating
old- and rose-cut diamonds
with cabochon-cut ruby eyes.
In the language of jewels,
the lizard symbolizes survival
and regeneration.

Title page. Theo Fennell combines
two of the most popular motifs
in men's jewelry – the skull and
the snake denoting rebirth
and eternity – in this blackened
18ct-gold right-hand ring
pavé set with rubies and
black diamonds.

Above. Cartier platinum and
18ct white-gold Panther clip
brooch. The panther, described
in single-cut diamonds, cabochon
sapphires and yellow-diamond
eyes, stands proud on a 152.35ct
Kashmir sapphire. The brooch
was made for the Duchess of
Windsor in 1949.

CONTENTS

FOREWORD

HH Sheikh Hamad bin Abdullah Al Thani

Today we associate the wearing of jewelry predominantly with women, but look back through history at different cultures around the world and you see that the fascination with gems and jewels originated with men.

In ancient times, and for centuries thereafter, beautiful stones and gems were considered an auspicious adornment for men. The wearing of jewelry on the head, around the neck or on the fingers was not only a symbol of power and wealth; it also possessed a greater meaning.

In coming to appreciate the beauty and craftsmanship of jewelry from all over the globe, I have also come to understand the deep significance of wearing jewels for mankind. Gems and stones were worn not just for their beauty and value, they also reflected one's aura, they had a cosmic meaning. Men wore specific gems and stones to balance their horoscopes, bring good health and bring protection to them and their families.

If you look back at the history of jewelry, for me there have been three creative peaks; three periods when the combination of design and craftsmanship have been of the highest calibre. First, there was a period during the Achaemenid Empire and Hellenistic period, from the sixth to the fourth centuries BCE, then a void for 2,000 years until the great Mughal Empire in India, from the sixteenth to the eighteenth century.

Finally, at the turn of the early twentieth century, there was a time of fusion between Indian and Western styles and techniques that culminated in art deco, when remarkable commissions were made by the great European jewelry houses for both maharajas and elite clients in the West.

My connection with James and this book came about on account of our shared appreciation for art deco, and I was delighted to agree to his request to include a painting from The Al Thani Collection, the stunning portrait of the Maharaja of Indore by Bernard Boutet de Monvel, reproduced in the Cartier profile. We also share a fascination with jewelry, its history and how wearing it is seen, by men in particular, as not only a symbol of power and wealth, but so much more besides.

I hope that this beautiful and fascinating book inspires in the reader an even greater interest in jewelry, an art form that I believe is rightfully considered a high point of human creative endeavour.

Tiger's Eye Turban Ornament (1937) created by Cartier for Maharaja Digvijaysinhji of Nawanagar and now in The Al Thani Collection. This masterpiece of art deco design features an exceptional 61.5 carat cognac-coloured diamond and epitomizes the creative dialogue between Indian princes and European jewelry houses in the early twentieth century.

PREFACE

> 'Jewelry is one of the things in which
> the best is always good enough.'
> Hardy Amies, *ABC of Men's Fashion* (1964)

A pair of platinum-on-gold art deco onyx cufflinks (c.1920) from Bentley & Skinner set with central old brilliant-cut diamonds and surrounded by a scalloped diamond border.

As the arbiter of English understatement, Hardy Amies rightly said in 1964, 'Jewelry for men is always dangerous ground. It is too dull merely to give the advice that it should be plain and expensive.' And yet that's the three-line whip that has been delivered by the men's style journals ever since. Some critics would have you believe that it is high treason to wear anything more ostentatious than a wristwatch and a family signet ring. But since 1964 declining dress codes have denuded the fashionable man of the opportunity, if not the inclination, to wear jewelry.

Few men outside royal circles wear white tie more than once a year, if ever, making gem-set dress studs and matching cufflinks unicorns of the men's jewelry box. Button-cuff shirts outsell French cuffs by four to one, making the link, however humble, an endangered species. Cravats are rarely seen outside a *Twilight* convention, spelling the end of the stick pin, and the gentle art of smoking has been vilified to the point that gold cigarette cases with cabochon-sapphire clasps are curios rather than necessities.

And yet men's desire to wear jewelry hasn't been so strong since the 1970s. It is a rare CEO or hedge-fund tycoon who doesn't wear a wristful of friendship bracelets that demonstrate a life outside finance. The Alphas of the species are already trading up to bracelets, signet rings and pendants in yellow gold. Important pieces of antique fine jewelry now appear on the red carpets, worn by tastemaking young actors and musicians such as Jared Leto, Pharrell Williams, Aldis Hodge and Alexander Skarsgård, who have not only revived classic dress studs and cufflinks, but also reinvented brooches, stick pins and chains as necklaces and lapel festoons.

Although we should applaud them for keeping the flame of fine jewelry alive, hip-hop swag and rock-star bling are in the process of being refined as actors, musicians and sports stars graduate from the nursery slope of jewelry for gentlemen. At the turn of the twenty-first century men wearing earrings were still considered common or comedic. Thanks to Cristiano Ronaldo, Will Smith, David Beckham and Lewis Hamilton, diamond ear studs have become an elegant addition to black tie.

Unlike female actors, who tend to borrow jewelry as red-carpet product placement, high-profile men buy their jewelry in a way that echoes India's maharajas, who invested the sovereign wealth in precious, portable property. The investment potential for fine men's jewelry is rock solid. According to a report by Bonhams auction house in January 2017, 'period and designer jewelry has outperformed the housing market over the past decade. Research reveals the rarest and most sought-after pieces of vintage jewelry have soared in value by over 80 per cent during the past ten years. By contrast, average house prices in England have risen in value by just 47 per cent in the same period of time.'

Jewelry for Gentlemen celebrates times and tastes past that modern men have adapted and restyled for the twenty-first century. It also showcases pieces of jewelry that will be future heirlooms, as made by modern masters Shaun Leane, Theo Fennell, David Yurman, Ara Vartanian, Solange Azagury-Partridge and Stephen Webster. These craftsmen and women are supplying a demand as well as inspiring a young generation hungry for new ways to wear men's jewelry.

Cartier, Tiffany & Co., Bulgari, Chaumet, Van Cleef & Arpels and Boucheron have all significantly increased their selection of fine jewelry for men, with dedicated sections on their websites for the boys. Cartier in particular has been most generous with the house archives, although the antique jewelry photographed for the book was kindly loaned by the London antiques dealers Bentley & Skinner, Hancocks, Lucas Rarities and Wartski. I have also been fortunate to work with the great London auction houses Sotheby's and Bonhams, who opened their picture archives from the last two decades of jewelry sales.

Although the antique market for men's jewelry is buoyant, masterpieces from the royal family of artistic jewelers – such as Fabergé, Lalique, Flato, Belperron, Verdura, Schlumberger, Grima, Hemmerle and JAR (Joel Arthur Rosenthal) – are relatively accessible for less than the price of a modest Patek Philippe watch. *Jewelry for Gentlemen* is filled with works by the world's most famous marques. For a collector, the signature of a great house is imperative at auction. But for a man who loves beautiful things, an unsigned piece that demonstrates artistry comparable to the historic marques will save an awful lot of money.

Ultimately, this book is about wearing, rather than investing in, fine men's jewelry. The intention is to show contemporary jewelry in the context of timeless men's tailoring, courtesy of Henry Poole & Co, Turnbull & Asser and Sir Tom Baker. The book also proposes that antique stick pins, dress studs and brooches can be reimagined in a modern context. Photographing on bespoke suits not only gives an idea of scale but will also, we hope, inspire men to see jewelry for gentlemen as wearable works of art.

The actor Alexander Skarsgård attends the Met Gala in New York in 2016, wearing an 18ct yellow-gold Cartier Juste un Clou pin in the lapel of his Louis Vuitton tuxedo.

INTRODUCTION

'One Spring in the Roaring Twenties, caskets of diamonds
journeyed from the Punjab to Paris in the luggage of one of the
most extravagant of the Indian maharajas. This was the prelude
to the creation of one of the most mythical pieces of jewelry
in contemporary history: the Maharaja of Patiala's necklace.'

Cartier, *Precious Stories of Diamonds* (2006)

As a brief canter around the British Museum will demonstrate, men
of power have adorned themselves with yellow gold and gemstones since
the time of the ancients. Celtic thanes, Egyptian pharaohs and Chinese
emperors all chose sartorial treasures to display their wealth, refinement
and status, and the artistry of the goldsmith invariably made the object
more highly prized than the intrinsic value of the precious metal and
stones. This remains true of the most desirable pieces of jewelry today.

The bejeweled male was a glorious if increasingly uncommon sight
until well into the twentieth century. In 1928 the fabulously wealthy
Maharaja Sir Bhupinder Singh of Patiala commissioned Cartier in Paris
to create a five-tier diamond-and-ruby festoon necklace to frame a
cushion-cut 234.6-carat yellow diamond. A photograph in the Cartier
archives shows Sir Bhupinder's son Maharaja Sir Yadavindra Singh
wearing the necklace in 1939, with a foliate diamond 'fender' tiara over
his turban. He also sports a substantial diamond rivière necklace and
a diamond starburst brooch pinned to a gold-embroidered coat, a
large diamond collar and a pearl drop earring. The Patiala necklace
disappeared after the Second World War, presumably sold and broken
up and the stones re-set, although Cartier reconstructed its masterpiece
with the original platinum frame and diamonds, and a citrine in place
of the yellow diamond.

Alas, the scale and dazzle of jewelry for men will most likely never
again touch such sublime ostentation. But the maharajas' spirit underpins
the choice of jewelry for gentlemen in this book. Fine jewelry for men is
a rarefied taste, and so wearing an exceptional ring, brooch or cufflink is
a statement as brave and unique in the twenty-first century as the Patiala
necklace was in the previous one.

For men who collect precious antique jewels, the most highly prized
sartorial treasure is the piece that holds all the following major cards: it
is signed by an important maker and was owned by a man of fascination,
and its design perfectly embodies the elegance of an era. A prime example
is the Duke of Windsor's Cartier art deco platinum-and-diamond dress

Above. The Patiala necklace,
also known as the Collier de
Patiala, was created by Cartier in
1928 for Maharaja Sir Bhupinder
Singh of Patiala. A total of 2,929
diamonds are placed in festoon
style framing the 234.6ct yellow
De Beers diamond.

Opposite. Maharaja Sir
Yadavindra Singh was the
last ruler of Patiala to wear
the necklace. Last seen intact
in 1948, it was subsequently
stripped of its major stones.
The De Beers diamond was
sold at Sotheby's Geneva
for nearly $3.2 million in 1982.

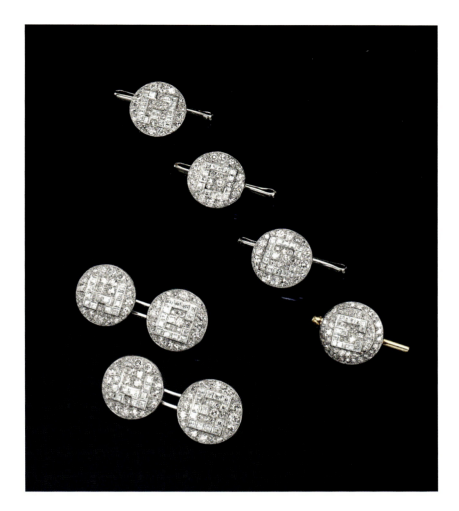

set of 1935, sold by Sotheby's in 2010. The Duke and Duchess of
Windsor's jewels had already broken the world record for a single-
owner jewelry sale when they were auctioned in 1987 for £31 million.

The dress set, comprising three buttons, a stud and cufflinks, is
monogrammed E (Edward) in diamonds, with an E and a W (Wallis) on
the links. One link is inscribed with a date (23/6/35) that was significant
for the lovers, and 'hold tight' is inscribed on another. The year 1935 was
pivotal in their love story. Within a year the Duke would be proclaimed
King Edward VIII and then abdicate for the love of Mrs Simpson. His
diamonds tell this story in miniature. The dress set belonging to an
ex-king adds lustre, as does the Duke's posthumous position as one of the
best-dressed men of the twentieth century. These elements contributed
to the £70,000–90,000 estimate for the set, leaping to £115,250 in 2010.

Any piece of jewelry connected to the doomed Russian Romanov royal
family is highly prized, to the point that they are collected and worn like
religious relics. Add the magic word Fabergé, the imperial jeweler that
was nationalized after the Russian Revolution in 1918, and even modest

pieces of men's jewelry and *objets de vertu* touched by the Romanovs soar into six figures.

In 2009 Sotheby's sold the 100-plus pieces of a forgotten cache of imperial jewels discovered hiding in pillowcases in a Stockholm bank vault belonging to the Grand Duchess Maria Pavlovna (a cousin of Tsar Nicholas II). An imperial enamel, two-colour-gold and diamond Fabergé cigarette case made in 1899 and bought by the Dowager Empress Maria Feodorovna contributed £577,250 to the total of £7,073,300. A handsome pair of Fabergé links in a concentric circular motif with a cabochon sapphire in the centre of each realized £17,500.

The late San Franciscan socialite and realtor John Traina's collection of sartorial treasures included Fabergé jade boxes, gold cigarette cases and fifty-three dress sets made by the greats: Van Cleef & Arpels, Harry Winston, Cartier, David Webb, Tiffany & Co. and Verdura. The 'Elegant John Traina' sale at Sotheby's New York in 2011 doubled estimates and realized $1,921,755. Traina's taste in twentieth-century cufflinks and dress studs was exquisite: 18ct yellow-gold and enamel frogs on lily pads

A Fabergé jeweled and two-colour gold-mounted silver cigarette case (St Petersburg, 1904), auctioned in Sotheby's sale 'Romanov Heirlooms: The Lost Inheritance of Grand Duchess Maria Pavlovna' in 2009 for £58,850 (from a high estimate of £2,500).

designed by David Well ($6,250), and Jean Schlumberger for Tiffany 18ct yellow-gold and haematite acorns ($6,250).

Traina is a hero of jewelry for gentlemen. One can imagine the pleasure he found in acquiring those dress sets, knowing full well that they would be an amusing opener to a conversation, as all good jewelry should be. Victorian men's jewelry was designed specifically to raise an inquisitive eyebrow questioning the story behind a diamond wishbone stick pin, an enamel playing-card cufflink or a jeweled horse-and-jockey lapel pin. The Victorians appreciated jewelry that hinted at a man's interests, character or heart. Sentiment is a theme that runs throughout this book, largely because so many pieces for men were precious mementos of interesting lives.

Jewelry for Gentlemen takes a pragmatic rather than a fantastical stance on the subject. All the pieces illustrated here are or have been for sale, and similar pieces can still be bought and worn. Very little pre-nineteenth-century men's jewelry survives outside museum collections, with the exception of Roman to Renaissance cameos and intaglios that have been consistently re-set as men's rings. Following is a brief guide to the key stylistic movements in jewelry design of the nineteenth and twentieth centuries, with notes on the marques that feature most prominently in this book.

Right. The 18ct yellow-gold and black Tahitian pearl Acorn cufflinks by Jean Schlumberger for Tiffany & Co. were his most popular design for men. The piece is still made by Tiffany, although the pearls have been replaced with haematite.

Archaeological Revival

Yellow gold in the antique style is unimpeachably masculine. The Castellani workshop in Rome produced jewelry inspired by the study of Byzantine, Greek and Roman gold archaeological finds. The **Castellani** brothers rediscovered the Etruscan technique of gold granulation, setting ancient cameos and intaglios in elaborate filigree designs. Jewelry made in the archaeological revival style was bought by Emperor Napoleon III of France and by Queen Victoria's consort, Prince Albert. **Carlo Giuliano** trained in the Castellani workshops, where he became a master of enamelling and developed his own style, rather than copying antiquities. The setting of ancient coins and cameos in yellow gold has since become a signature of the Italian house Bulgari (right).

Above. This 18ct yellow-gold Bulgari cufflinks and dress-studs set with coins dating from the fifth century BC was auctioned for $13,750 in Sotheby's 'Elegant John Traina' sale in 2011.

Below. Rare gold-and-enamel cufflinks by Lalique Paris (c.1900), painted with the face of the wine god Bacchus within *plique-á-jour* leaves and opaque enamel grapes, were auctioned in Sotheby's 'Romanov Heirlooms' sale in 2009 for £37,250.

Art Nouveau

The languid lines of art nouveau jewelry acknowledge the influence of Japanese art, the Aesthetic movement and natural motifs. Art nouveau revolutionized jewelry design and the master was **René Lalique** (below), whose intricate work was characterized by renderings of flowers, vines and the female form in gossamer-thin yellow gold and sinuous plique-á-jour enamelwork. Lalique's Parisian contemporaries **Georges Fouquet** and **Henri Vever** mastered the art, as did **Liberty & Co** in London and the American marques **Tiffany & Co.** and **Marcus & Co**.

Naturalistic

The 1890s vogue for naturalistic motifs in white diamonds and coloured stones unleashed a swarm of jeweled bees, butterflies, spiders, lizards, dragonflies and birds in flight, some set *en tremblant* to move with the wearer. Spray brooches of ivy, orchids, wisteria and roses were also popular. Naturalistic brooches by **Tiffany & Co.**, **Chaumet** and **Garrard**, among others, are a particularly rich source for men's lapel pins. Diamond hair ornaments for belle époque ladies migrate happily on to the lapel of a modern gentleman.

Above. A naturalistic Victorian diamond butterfly brooch from Bentley & Skinner set with round old brilliant-cut diamonds (11ct) set in silver to a yellow-gold backing with cabochon-cut ruby eyes.

Right. A belle époque diamond brooch (c.1910) designed as three intertwined foliate hoops set with old brilliant- and rose-cut diamonds cased by Le Roy et Fils.

Garland Style

Looking back to eighteenth-century Rococo tastes, the garland style of jewelry prevalent in the first two decades of the twentieth century was distinctive for its lightness and shimmer. Fretworking in platinum gave setters the opportunity to make the precious but strong metal appear as fragile as lace (below). New cutting and polishing techniques introduced the baguette, trapeze, marquise and triangular cuts for stones, as well as sharpening the briolette, brilliant, rose, pear and cabochon techniques. The garland style – loops, swags, bows and tassels – was led by **Cartier**, **LaCloche Frères**, **Chaumet** and **Fabergé**. Today the lacework platinum setting of white diamonds is a speciality of the Italian house of **Buccellati**.

Art Deco

The frantic energy of art deco was reflected in fashion and jewelry influenced by the *Garçonne* style of Coco Chanel's moderns, Serge Diaghilev's Ballets Russes and the craze for Egyptiana following the discovery of Tutankhamun's tomb in 1922. The East-meets-West ebullience of the maharajas' jewels made by **Cartier**, **Boucheron** and **Van Cleef & Arpels** arguably represented the apex of the era's style. Art deco jewelry is georic in design and has a cold, severe brilliance. The dazzle of precious stones is balanced by the dull sheen of lacquer, onyx and rock crystal. Deco had its mavericks who retained their own style throughout the period, such as **Paul Flato**, for whom **Fulco di Verdura** designed the ingenious solid yellow-gold Nuts & Bolts cufflinks, and **Suzanne Belperron**, who graduated from the **René Boivin** atelier in Paris.

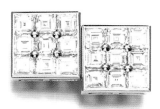

Clockwise from left. Platinum square-terminal art deco Cartier cufflinks set with square diamonds and joined by a curb-link chain; 1930s baton-designed Cartier sapphire-and-diamond cufflinks with calibré-cut sapphire terminals; a single-cut and baguette-cut diamond double-clip brooch (c.1930s) signed Drayson.

Mid-Century Opulence

Of the limited jewelry design during the Second World War, the most interesting pieces for men are the yellow-gold 'tank track' and 'bicycle chain' bracelets designed by **Cartier**. The spotlight after the war turned towards the American masters **Harry Winston**, **Tiffany & Co.** and **Fulco di Verdura**. Post-war austerity had already popularized semi-precious stones, which are particularly showy set in yellow-gold signet rings. Novelty brooches such as those by **Van Cleef & Arpels** and **LaCloche Frères**, and **Verdura**'s 'cocktail jewelry' entered the men's jewelry box with such talking-point pieces as **Jean Schlumberger for Tiffany & Co.**'s rope knot, acorn and animal cufflinks.

Futurism and Abstraction

The stars of 1960s and 1970s jewelry, **Andrew Grima**, **John Donald** and **David Webb**, have a cult following among connoisseurs of fine jewelry design, and Grima is venerated and collected by such tastemakers as Miuccia Prada, Marc Jacobs and the Duke and Duchess of Devonshire. There was a space-age, 1960s futurist element to Grima's preference for included, unpolished minerals, crystals and semi-precious stones. Precious stones are accents in Grima's designs, and among his most covetable work are the stalactite and shell brooches in woven yellow gold with chips of baguette-cut diamonds.

Above, left. *Cartier Fleur Ouvrante* textured gold brooch (c.1960s) with hinged petals that open to reveal *en tremblant* diamonds and coloured gemstones.

Above, right. A diamond brooch by John Donald (1972) with openwork crown of 18ct white and yellow gold and spokes of varying lengths terminating in brilliant-cut diamond finials.

Overleaf, clockwise from left. A Fabergé pierced diamond bow brooch (c.1913) millegrain set in platinum with rose-cut diamonds and a central brilliant-cut diamond. Courtesy of Bentley & Skinner; Carl Fabergé reeded platinum ball cufflinks (c.1896–1908) surmounted by cabochon blue-star sapphires, heightened with rose diamonds; a pair of lilac guilloché enamel and diamond-set cufflinks by Carl Fabergé, St Petersburg, c.1885. Courtesy of Wartski.

CHAPTER ONE

RINGS

—

RINGS

'Look, how my ring encompasseth thy finger.
Even so thy breast encloseth my poor heart;
Wear both of them, for both of them are thine.'
William Shakespeare, *Richard III*

In certain circles a man is judged as much by the placement of his rings as by their design. A wedding band is traditionally worn on the fourth finger of the left hand, and the signet ring on the left-hand little finger. There are those who say a gentleman will wear only this precise configuration and nothing more. It does not, however, pay to heed such absolutes. Prince Charles, for example, wears his gold intaglio signet ring carved with the Prince of Wales's feathers and motto *Ich dien* ('I serve') on his little finger with his Welsh gold wedding ring made by Wartski stacked beneath. It is a pleasing arrangement that follows the precedent of his father and grandfather, the Duke of Edinburgh and King George VI.

Queen Victoria's sons, the princes Albert Edward, Alfred, Arthur and Leopold, wore towers of rings denoting love, loyalty, mourning and friendship on their left-hand little fingers. The precedent was set by the queen herself, who in later life wore more rings than Liberace. None of the rings worn by the royal males in the 1860s and 1870s was a wedding band: the exchange of wedding rings between man and wife did not become mainstream until after the Second World War.

The Duke of Windsor helped to set a fashion for stacked men's rings that endures today. Cartier's Trinity three-colour-gold interlocking hoop ring (1924) is one of the house's most successful designs for men. The Duke (as Prince of Wales) wore a yellow-, white- and rose-gold Trinity inscribed 'Darling Wallis' on his little finger throughout his courtship of Mrs Simpson in the 1930s. The House of Windsor offers a useful perspective on the narrow rules that discourage men from wearing anything more adventurous than a plain wedding band.

If the wedding ring is a relative arriviste in the jewel box, the yellow-gold oval signet ring hand-engraved with a crest, insignia, initial or talisman in reverse is as old as civilization, dating back 4,000 years to ancient Egypt. And yet a fourteenth-century BC solid-gold signet ring carved deeply with the hieroglyph of Tutankhamun could pass unnoticed in the jewelry section of Dover Street Market.

The techniques of carving intaglio designs into the flat bezel of a solid-gold ring are timeless. The principle is exactly the same whether it is a signet ring made for a fifteenth-century Florentine Medici banker or

Page 22. The model Lucky Blue Smith at Paris Fashion Week in 2016, wearing pieces from the Israeli-born, New York-based Eli Halili's fine jewelry collection. Smith has popularized the layering of many pieces of men's jewelry for the Instagram generation.

Opposite. The Duke of Windsor wears Cartier's Trinity ring at Government House in Nassau, the Bahamas.

Below. Cartier's Trinity ring, made from 18ct gold in three colours (yellow, white and rose), was patented in 1924.

Opposite. One of ten surviving signet rings made by Nitot (now Chaumet) in 1810 for Emperor Napoleon I to give on the occasion of his wedding to Empress Marie-Louise. The emperor's cipher is surrounded with thirty-seven brilliant-cut diamonds.

Below. This nineteenth-century hessonite garnet cameo of the Roman Emperor Tiberius was auctioned by Bonhams in 2014 for £6,000.

a twenty-first-century partner at Deloitte. The pleasure of having a gold family ring made is best described by Emmet Smith, director of the Hatton Garden workshop Rebus, whose craftsmen specialize in signet rings. 'With a hand-engraved message or symbol, an object can be transformed from the ordinary into the extraordinary,' he says, 'giving it a life and meaning of its own, and in time the item will acquire its own personality.' The modern heraldry Rebus is crafting has liberated such rings from the taint of being considered suburban.

The liberation of the signet ring has revived the most collected design in the history of men's jewelry. It has also brought a new set of customers for antique gold signet rings set with intaglio hardstones or precious gems. Julius Caesar, Pope Paul II, Lorenzo de' Medici, Louis Philippe d'Orléans, Emperor Napoleon I and J. P. Morgan all amassed famous collections of carved gemstone rings. The appeal of such pieces has crossed continents and centuries.

The ancient Greeks and Romans carved carnelian, bloodstone, onyx, jasper, amethyst and ruby with portrait medallions of gods, emperors, heroes, sacred birds or animals and protective symbols. From the first century BC, when Emperor Augustus founded the Claudian dynasty, seal rings depicting the imperial family were sent to all corners of the Roman Empire to establish each reign. Authenticated intaglio portraits of heroes of the ancient world light up today's auction rooms. In 2011 a 200 BC gold-and-carnelian intaglio of Alexander the Great sold for £55,200 at Bonhams, and in 2014 a first- or second-century AD ring depicting Emperor Augustus' scheming consort Livia posing as the goddess Ceres sold for £25,000.

'The bejeweled hand denoting power and strength reached a peak in the Renaissance with Henry VIII's table-cut ruby knuckledusters, as painted by Hans Holbein the Younger.'

One of the most self-indulgent men's jewelry purchases is the characterful right-hand ring. It is worn on the little finger, a position that separates it from the wedding and signet on the left and allows a more elaborate jewel to stand alone. When a man's ring is exceptional – and what's the point of wearing one that isn't? – the 'one ring per hand' rule makes sense.

The bejeweled hand denoting power and strength reached a peak in the Renaissance with Henry VIII's table-cut ruby knuckledusters, as painted by Hans Holbein the Younger. They were part of a parure of rubies in yellow gold that decorated Henry's doublet, sleeves and cap. Renaissance-style gold rings framing a large coloured gemstone are a precedent that can be smuggled into the twenty-first century, albeit one per hand rather than one per finger like Bluff King Hal.

The American jeweler David Yurman's men's collection, designed by his son Evan, has a Henrician sensibility for right-hand rings such as a faceted garnet set in yellow gold and a carved carnelian scarab set in a 22ct yellow-gold oval (see page 160). London-based Stephen Webster's rings are equally powerful, with a heraldic Renaissance swagger. His yellow-gold Kabuki mask motif with cabochon-ruby eyes and diamond accents looks like a gargoyle. Webster is unafraid to set (and sell) a substantial bloodstone or whisky quartz as large as Henry's rubies in a right-hand ring, or to carve a memento mori engraved yellow-gold skull ring from a citrine with diamond eyes.

Preceding pages, left. A copy of the lost Holbein the Younger portrait of King Henry VIII (1536–37) executed for the Palace of Whitehall. The king wears one of several parures of jewelry: a set of table-cut ruby buttons, rings and a magnificent collar mounted in yellow gold.

Preceding pages, right. Evan Yurman, design director of David Yurman, owns a handsome Fortune collection faceted garnet ring set in 18ct yellow gold that echoes the gravitas and glory of Henry VIII's ruby rings, none of which survive in the Royal Collection.

Opposite, clockwise from top left. A yellow-gold, pavé-diamond and cabochon-ruby Japanese Warrior Mask ring designed and personally owned by Stephen Webster; Shaun Leane's 18ct yellow-gold and enamel Thorn & Heart signet ring; the Lionheart ring from Solange Azagury-Partridge's 'Alpha' collection in 18ct blackened yellow gold set with diamond eyes and a ruby heart; the Villain ring from the same collection, a cabochon emerald set in 18ct blackened yellow gold.

Left. A Roman carnelian intaglio of a nude male from the Ceres collection sold by Bonhams London in 2014 for £1,875.

'Hip hop, gay marriage and gangster style have all opened the door for diamonds by day, and contemporary jewelers are refining the aesthetic to appeal to all men, rather than to style tribes.'

Above. Wright & Teague's Naga serpent ring in 18ct yellow gold.

Opposite, top. The 18ct white-gold and diamond Quill ring designed and personally owned by Shaun Leane.

Opposite, bottom. The Muz ring in 18ct blackened yellow gold and diamonds from Solange Azagury-Partridge's 'Alpha' collection.

Theo Fennell is the maestro of full-voltage jewels with a Renaissance sensibility. The skull, cross, key and heraldic beasts are all motifs that he returns to. His interpretation of the memento mori skull for a right-hand men's ring is a three-dimensional pavé-set diamond beauty with a twining snake that stands proud on the finger (see page 2).

Solange Azagury-Partridge's 'Alpha' collection of men's jewelry is a lesson in balancing precious stones and precious metals. The collection uses 18ct blackened gold, which fades to reveal the glimmer of yellow metal beneath. The technique makes the ruby and diamond set into her Lionheart ring shine out of the darkness. The showpiece is the 18ct gold Villain ring set with a large cabochon emerald. The stone is included, so it smoulders rather than shines.

Hip hop, gay marriage and gangster style have all opened the door for diamonds by day, and contemporary jewelers are refining the aesthetic to appeal to all men, rather than to style tribes. Shaun Leane creates jewelry with a nobility and beauty that makes it hard to classify as men's or women's. His interlocking rings have a savage beauty that speaks to men. One of his most successful designs for men, a ring that he wears personally, is a white-gold grille design featuring bars set with perfectly matched white diamonds standing off the cage of the ring (see opposite and page 74).

Commissioning a ring from a contemporary maker has the obvious advantage that you are collaborating on a unique piece that will probably be passed down. The proportion and fit will be right for you, and an idea from a women's collection can be adapted to suit the proportions of a man's hand. The same cannot be said for signed antique pieces, and indeed it would be the height of folly to resize an important antique ring.

Scouting for antique dress rings for men can be a minefield. Nineteenth- and twentieth-century women's rings are available in the antiques market, and slip easily onto the little finger. Late nineteenth-century half-hoop yellow-gold rings set with three matching stones also look elegant and substantial on a man's hand. The half-hoop design shows a lot of stone and minimal setting, and sits close to the finger. The half-hoop trinity was an incredibly popular design made for all pockets, so you will find them in antiques shops, set with semi-precious stones.

The gems in a half-hoop ring were said to have meaning, which you may choose to believe or not. In the lapidary language, amethysts traditionally protected the wearer against drunkenness, making the stone particularly popular for men's rings. In 1913 Tiffany & Co.'s gem expert George Kunz wrote *The Curious Lore of Precious Stones*, in which he explained that rings set with certain stones had various talismanic properties. If gemstones delivered on all the promises he made for them, they would put doctors and psychiatrists out of business. Superstitions become traditions; but when the finest jewelers in the world go against received wisdom, it is time to ask whether certain rules are outdated.

It is still frowned on to mix white and yellow precious metal, but the advantage of a piece such as the Cartier Trinity ring is to open up every item in a jewel box, should a man wish to match ring to links or tie stud. Boucheron's Quatre Classique (designed by Azagury-Partridge) is a handsome tower of 18ct yellow, white and pink gold with a band of dark 'tile-effect' ceramic that gives a masculine edge.

New materials and finishes that have proved popular in men's jewelry include ceramic (a material Stephen Webster has used to great effect) and plating gold with rhodium, a brittle, mirror-like metal. Chaumet interpreted its Liens ring – a three-quarter band held together by a stitch of diamond-set white gold – in a thick band of black ceramic that makes the perfect men's dress ring, worn on the little finger. Cartier produced a rhodium-plated white-gold version of one of its chicest and most simple designs, Juste un Clou, a nail of precious metal that bends around the finger or the wrist.

It is heartening that the Panthère de Cartier, introduced by the house in 1914 and much beloved by the Duchess of Windsor (whose Panthère bracelet sold at Sotheby's for £4,521,250 in 2010), has now prowled into the men's collection with a fabulous yellow-gold roaring panther's head embellished with lacquer, peridots and onyx. Even more dazzling is the Panthère men's ring set with diamonds, onyx and emerald eyes. Granted, a certain chutzpah is required to wear it, but one doesn't imagine the men on the Forbes list are lacking in confidence or self-belief.

Above. The Panthère de Cartier 18ct white-gold ring set with 365 brilliant-cut diamonds, emerald eyes and onyx.

Opposite. In this portrait from 1925, Tamara de Lempicka paints a suitably angular, futurist emerald ring on the finger of her lover the Marquis de Sommi, an aristocrat-musician.

ARA VARTANIAN

'There is a fine line between a cool piece of jewelry for a guy and bling.'

The Brazilian-born jewelry designer Ara Vartanian works in the tradition of the brothers Jacques and Pierre Cartier, travelling the world to find rare gemstones and designing unique pieces to romance them. Vartanian is an innovator who has made inverted diamond settings a signature, with a preference for black, smoky grey and brown diamonds over the sparkle of a brilliant-cut white. He chooses to sell only in his boutiques in São Paulo and Rio di Janeiro, as well as his off-radar London flagship in Bruton Place, Mayfair.

Male clients feel instantly at ease in the Bruton Place bunker. A vast scalloped concrete wall installed by Estúdio Tupi architects shields the shop from public view, and the vibe inside is 1960s Palm Springs Modern with vintage vinyl, Japanese whisky and jewelry displayed in what look like fish tanks in a Bond villain's lair. Vartanian wears his jewelry as lightly as a politician's conscience: a leather pendant strung with black-diamond beads, his talismanic Mandala pendant set with inverted black diamonds, an 18ct yellow-gold open-fanged Shark ring and an extraordinary silver belt set with inverted black diamonds with a marquise-cut diamond on the buckle. The belt is part of a twenty-five-piece collection designed with his muse and mentor Kate Moss.

Vartanian met the model and tastemaker Moss in Brazil in 2012, and credits her with removing the boundaries between jewelry for men and for women. 'We didn't think about sex at all,' he says. 'I might be wearing a ring or pendant that Kate wears in her own way. It is equally boring to think about gay or straight jewelry. There's no such thing. What I love about working with Kate is her creative mind. She's not a physical designer, but it is a meeting of minds.' Vartanian shows a prototype string bracelet set with a collection of substantial inverted stones. This is a precious piece of jewelry with a relaxed attitude and beachside charm.

'As a designer, I have a creative path,' says Vartanian, who is so aware of legacy that he documents every design, presuming that in twenty years' time it will appear at auction. 'A collaboration is a pause along that path that relaxes the mind and opens up new possibilities.' The fact that the pieces are polysexual adds to the edginess of the creative pairing with Moss. 'I do think British men are more willing to go there with jewelry,' he says. 'It always makes me laugh that my friends in Brazil are quite prepared to wear Speedos but they are reluctant to wear a piece of jewelry. Hilarious! That said, I am seeing more and more men's jewelry now, and that goes for rock 'n' roll Brazilian guys in their sixties as much as for the kids.'

Vartanian's fine jewelry is an easy sell to men because it is designed by a guy who has an equal passion for motorbikes and cars. His silver Nuts & Bolts cufflinks

Above. This inverted black-diamond pendant is a variation on an Ara Vartanian design made exclusively for the jeweler, Kate Moss and Rolling Stone Ronnie Wood.

Opposite. Ara Vartanian photographed at his Mayfair flagship in Bruton Place, London.

Above. Ara Vartanian's sterling
silver Nuts & Bolts cufflinks.

Opposite and overleaf, right.
Vartanian says of his new work:
'Fashion and fine jewelry see
the emergence of ungendered
design: style without gender,
style for both sexes, style that
unites the sexes.'

Overleaf, left. Ara Vartanian's
18ct white-gold Shark ring set
with black diamonds.

are the most obvious reflection of that, and
echo Verdura's yellow-gold interpretation
for Flato. But Vartanian claims never to
look at other jewelers' work past or present.
Pieces in his fine jewelry portfolio that
speak to men include an 18ct yellow-gold
bracelet with inverted black and white
diamond terminals, his Shark ring, pavé
set with black diamonds, the 18ct white-
gold Jagged ring and an 18ct yellow-
gold inverted black-diamond eternity
ring. Even his signature Hook earrings –
an ingenious design that hooks above the
lobe, allowing the weight of a drop earring
to balance without stretching the lobe –
could look sharp in neat hooks of black
or white diamonds.

'Men have bought two-finger rings,'
says Vartanian of another signature that
distributes an even line of gemstones
across two or three fingers with comfort.
His Octopus two-finger ring, with a large
stone and pavé-diamond-set tentacles,
has all the hallmarks of a right-hand dress
ring. 'I don't wear jewelry to look rock 'n'
roll or to look aesthetically more beautiful,'

he says. 'For me, jewelry is about the
memories of the people who gave it to
you and the power of the gemstones: for
protection, for good energy and as amulets.'

Vartanian's way of sourcing stones
personally, sitting down to sketch around
the jewel then overseeing staff in his
workshop as they realize his dreams is
increasingly rare in a jewelry business
flooded by fashion brands and dilettantes
posing as artisans. 'Everything we produce
is made in my workshops,' he says, 'and
the DNA of every piece is on paper. This is
important to my clients.' Vartanian's clients
are a family – albeit a glamorous one
that includes Patti Hansen, Ronnie Wood,
Naomi Campbell and Gisele Bündchen –
and he gets together with them socially
and professionally in New York, London
and São Paulo. It is no stretch of the
imagination to say that Vartanian's
aesthetic will surely move jewelry for
gentlemen to an unprecedented level.

www.aravartanian.com

LUCAS RARITIES

'Why should people pay millions and millions of pounds for fine art and not appreciate jewelry in the same way? I really believe jewelry should be seen as art; not just something that is worn as an adornment or badge of social status.'

Sam Loxton

Antique jewelers have in the past had the reputation of being a rather dry, humourless cabal robbing distressed dowagers of family heirlooms. The market has since caught fire, after the record-breaking Sotheby's sale of the Duchess of Windsor's jewels in 1987, when £31 million was realized for 300 pieces. When Sotheby's collected only twenty of the Windsor jewels for a second sale in 2010, it touched £8 million. Christie's shattered the auction record for a single-owner sale in 2011, when Elizabeth Taylor's 'Hollywood crown jewels' sold for £74.9 million.

The heat surrounding important antique jewelry has forged a young generation of high-profile, international dealers such as Lee Siegelson of Siegelson in New York, Cyrus and Rhianna Shennum's Bell and Bird in Austin, Texas, and London-based Martin Travis (Symbolic & Chase) and Sam Loxton (Lucas Rarities). They travel the world to discover treasures buried in the most unlikely places, and examine auction catalogues for unattributed orphans.

'Finding an important piece of jewelry is the highlight of my job, but it is getting harder every year,' says Loxton, who began as a porter in the jewelry department of Christie's while studying gemology. His eye for individual marques was honed tagging tens of thousands of pieces in advance of Christie's sales. His reputation was made when he attributed one of the most important pieces of art deco jewelry in history. He saw the unattributed 70ct carved emerald aigrette, embellished with a pronged tiara of diamonds, sapphires and pearls set in platinum, at a provincial auction house in Dorset. Loxton came to the conclusion that it was designed by Paul Iribe, and was one of the first Parisian masterpieces inspired by Paul Poiret's Orientalist couture and the Ballets Russes' notorious production of *Schéhérazade* in 1910. It is now a star piece in the Qatari Al Thani collection of 'Mughal to Maharaja' jewels, and has been displayed at the Metropolitan Museum of Art in New York, the Victoria and Albert Museum in London and the Grand Palais in Paris.

Lucas Rarities operates from a discreet suite of rooms above one of Mayfair's quieter streets. Established in 1999 as a London office for the Munich jeweler and gem merchant Ernst Färber (founded 1692), the firm was placed on the map by Loxton's spectacular find. He has been a director since 2007 and, with his right-hand woman Francesca Martin-Gutierrez, he literally searches the world for the finest examples of Boivin, Flato, Schlumberger, Sterlé and Fouquet, which he sells at showcases in Paris, New York, Los Angeles, London and Miami.

Above. This carved emerald turban ornament designed in 1911 by Paul Iribe is thought to be the first jewel to anticipate high art deco style.

Opposite. A 14ct yellow-gold, diamond and ruby Bow & Arrow brooch, attributed to Paul Flato.

'It is curious to see how men buying for women respond to jewelry. There's a vicarious pleasure that suggests to me an appetite for men's gem-set jewelry.'

Sam Loxton

Opposite. Exceptional white-gold, moonstone and diamond belle époque dress studs by Chaumet.

Below. Paul Flato's Deaf & Dumb cufflinks, made in the 1930s, were designed to spell out the wearer's initials.

Lucas Rarities appeals particularly to male collectors because an intelligent edit has been made by Loxton, quality and provenance assured. 'It is curious to see how men buying for women respond to jewelry,' he says. 'There's a vicarious pleasure that suggests to me an appetite for men's gem-set jewelry.' His area of expertise is fine jewelry designed between 1910 and 1970, but he also acquires pieces by contemporary jewelers such as JAR and Solange Azagury-Partridge, who are already acknowledged in museum collections and have a presence on the secondary market.

'The great jewelers were all revolutionary for their time,' says Loxton. 'When you're assessing an antique piece, it has to be well-manufactured, have a minimum of repair, an interesting provenance and ideally but not exclusively be designed by somebody important. The piece must also appeal instinctively.' As its name suggests, Lucas Rarities deals in antique jewelry with wit, beauty and masterly technique. 'The emphasis now is on quality,' says Loxton. 'I think people are finally appreciating that a piece doesn't need to be signed or unique to be a great piece of jewelry.'

'Most of my clients know about the designers and what questions to ask, but men do respond to the romance of a jewel. If they see me wearing a lapel pin at a fair like LAPADA, the seed that they can go further than a cufflink or a ring is sown.'

Sam Loxton

Paul Flato's yellow-gold Deaf & Dumb cufflinks are a fundamental addition to a collector's jewel box, as are the later Flato yellow-gold hand brooches for the lapel, embellished with pavé-set diamond bracelets and rings. Loxton's personal collection contains more than fifty cufflinks, and he has an eye for exceptional designs. He has sold extraordinary sets, such as a pair of 18ct yellow-gold onyx baton links by Tiffany & Co., a Cartier design of ribbed 18ct yellow-gold buds embedded with cabochon sapphires, a French 18ct yellow-gold design set with a colour drift of citrine lozenges, and a 24ct textured yellow-gold bar by Marianne Ostler, set with four sapphires.

Loxton is his own most effective model, and invariably wears Lucas Rarities links at the LAPADA antiques fair in London, as well as the occasional watch chain or stick pin, such as a magnificent yellow-and-rose-gold art nouveau rondel designed by Wiese. 'Most of my clients know about the designers and what questions to ask,' he says, 'but men do respond to the romance of a jewel. If they see me wearing a lapel pin at a fair like LAPADA, the seed that they can go further than a cufflink or a ring is sown.'

One of Lucas Rarities' most successful brooches for men is a set produced by Mellerio in the 1950s. Mellerio (founded 1613) is the oldest jeweler in Europe, and from 1777 had the patronage of Queen Marie Antoinette. Loxton's Mellerio brooches are twin crescents made in platinum and yellow gold with diamond-studded terminals. Another set that can be worn singly or as a pair is a Maison Boivin 18ct yellow-gold leaf design made in 1938, one set with diamonds and the other with cabochon rubies, sapphires and emeralds. One of the most graphic lapel-pin designs comes courtesy of Paul Flato: a 14ct yellow-gold V brooch embedded with sapphires and rubies that was made in 1945 to celebrate America's victory in the Second World War. Says Loxton, 'the greatest test for a piece of jewelry is how it feels in the hand. It might sound clichéd, but it is fascinating to think of the people who have held it before, and to see that it is so well made, that the jewel has withstood the test of time.'

www.lucasrarities.com

Opposite, top. Paul Flato's 14ct yellow-gold, sapphire, ruby and diamond V for Victory brooch of 1945.

Opposite, bottom. These Van Cleef & Arpels 18ct yellow-gold baton cufflinks with calibré-cut sapphire girdle date from about 1950.

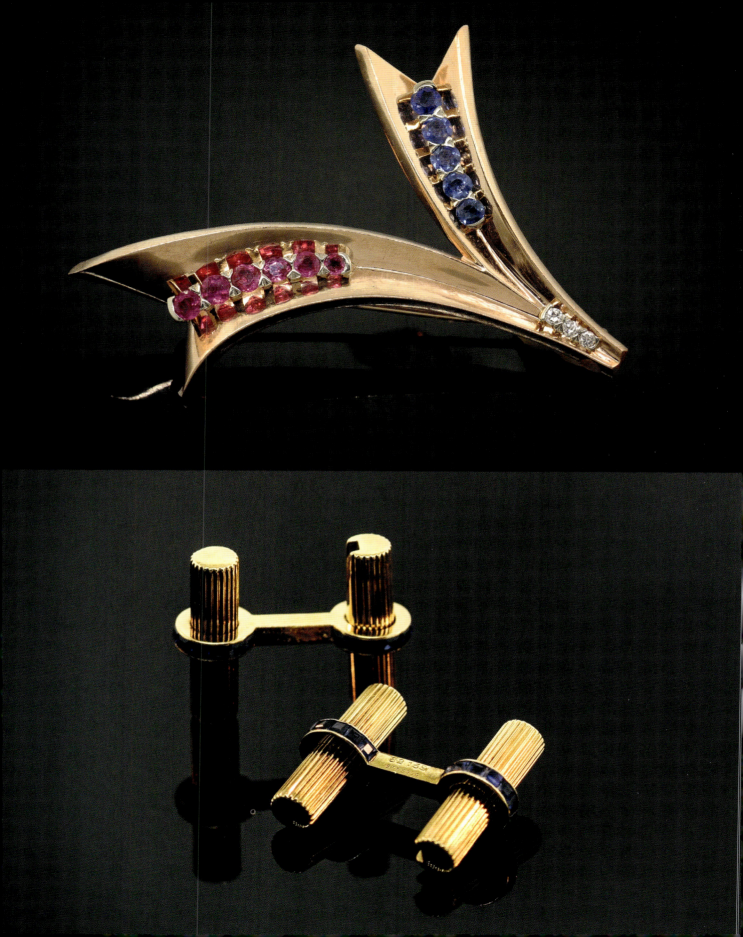

THEO FENNELL

'We make extraordinary things for extraordinary men.'

The charismatic British jewelry designer Theo Fennell is in the unique position of having 75 per cent of his business bespoke and commissioned by an international clientele, weighted equally towards men and women. The staff in his workshop above the Fulham Road flagship in London are, in his words, 'like an orchestra that can play anything', and his sketchbooks are filled with designs that could not be created under one roof anywhere else in London. It is not unusual for a single jewel in his workshop to pass through the hands of a dozen masters in stone-carving, setting, enamelling, engraving and hand-painting.

Fennell, an Etonian who apprenticed with the Hatton Garden silversmith Edward Barnard and Sons (est. 1680), established his business in 1982 and has moved beyond attempts to hallmark him as 'king of bling' or 'jeweler to the stars'. He is one of the few contemporary designers whose work appears in museum collections and at auction in the company of such historic artist jewelers as Flato, Verdura and Belperron.

'Men are getting bolder and there's a new level of peacockery that's rather satisfying,' says Fennell, who had the fortune to come up as the pink pound started to flex its muscles and the metrosexual male began to appreciate fine jewelry. 'Two decades ago it would be unheard of for a man to wear a solitaire diamond earring,' he says, 'but clients like David Beckham have made diamonds perfectly acceptable for men.' The motifs for which Fennell is famed – the cross, the key, the skull, the bee – all resonate with men and translate into dress rings, pendants, cufflinks and lapel pins.

Fennell's jewelry tells stories. His 18ct yellow-gold stable-door cufflinks flip open to reveal a portrait of a favourite thoroughbred. A black-gold and black-diamond bracelet (made for a Middle Eastern client) is etched with the skyline of his favourite cities, and portals behind the diamonds open to reveal miniatures of his nearest and dearest. A collection of ingenious open rings – 'to be worn in the spirit of the seventeenth century, and not for shrinking violets' – flip to reveal micro-sculpted secrets. A cabochon rubellite surrounded by diamonds and set in white gold featuring entwined magpie motifs flips to reveal a nest of yellow gold with opalite eggs and diamonds within.

Fennell's most extraordinary contemporary work is a series (collected by Elton John, among others) of jeweled, enamelled yellow-gold *Sic transit gloria mundi* masterwork brooches depicting monarchs such as Henry V, Henry VIII, Elizabeth I and Marie Antoinette with their faces carved as mammoth bone skulls. This is jewelry uniquely identified with the wearer and that gives an element of immortality when passed down.

Above. The Theo Fennell Bee Different 18ct yellow-gold stick pin, set with a 0.73ct pear-cut green tourmaline.

Opposite. An 18ct yellow-gold, diamond and enamel dress set made in the grand Fabergé tradition by Theo Fennell.

'If you're wearing a £350,000 watch, it is only there to give an indication of how you'd like to be perceived in a world that knows its value. A lot of branded jewelry built around large stones has the same effect.'

Opposite and below. Theo Fennell's *Sic transit gloria mundi* King Henry VIII and King Henry V masterwork brooches are made from 18ct yellow and white gold, diamonds, carved mammoth ivory, gemstones and enamel.

Overleaf, clockwise from top left. A 42.6ct Gemfields sugarloaf emerald opening ring hand-engraved and enamelled, with sculpted kissing frogs on lily pads inside; 18ct yellow-gold and lemon-quartz luminescent halogen light-bulb cufflinks; hand-carved intaglio smoky-quartz skull *Memento mori* cufflinks set in 18ct yellow gold with pavé-diamond accents; 18ct white-gold frogs on 18ct yellow-gold lily-pad cufflinks.

'If you're wearing a £350,000 watch, it is only there to give an indication of how you'd like to be perceived in a world that knows its value,' says Fennell. 'A lot of branded jewelry built around large stones has the same effect. For me, wearing a piece of jewelry that has a story brings a deeper conversation.' His position in the jewelry world is not dissimilar to that of the Florentine craftsmen making for the Medici in the sixteenth century. 'With patronage comes responsibility,' he says. 'Wherever wealth lies at any given point in history, it is a sign of a refined sensibility to patronize craftsmen and commission beautiful objects.'

Humour is another aspect of Fennell's work. Wives and girlfriends rarely feature, but Ferraris, villas, yachts and vistas have all been hand-painted in miniature and concealed behind hinged windows and portals as cufflinks. In one dramatic open ring, a portrait of Oscar Wilde is surrounded by diamonds and the band decorated with motifs inspired by Aubrey Beardsley's illustrations of *Salome*. The shank flips open to reveal a portrait of Wilde's young lover Lord Alfred 'Bosie' Douglas, with the inscription 'the love that dare not speak its name'. It is 'not everyday wear', as Fennell remarks.

Putting flesh on the bone of the skull rings, Fennell's series of Heroes and Villains rings in yellow and white gold and silver have become cult. Elvis Presley, Marilyn Monroe, Mao Tse-Tung, Lenin, Che Guevara, Eva Perón and Winston Churchill have all been cast as substantial three-dimensional right-hand rings and occasionally twinned as cufflinks, as with Bob Marley and Nelson Mandela. Whimsy is as important as sentimentality when aiming for the heart of a dedicated collector.

Fennell doesn't scale down when designing for men, or rein in an idea when it has more to give. His rock-crystal light-bulb cufflinks set in yellow gold that glow in the right light are ingenious and amusing. They are catnip to a collector; who will yearn for the matching dress-stud sets. Similarly, a white-diamond pavé-set skull ring will trigger the desire for the links and the dress studs. In some respects, the showroom is a laboratory that inspires the bespoke customers to think even bigger.

'It is incredible to me that even two decades ago, wearing hair gel was considered effeminate,' says Fennell. 'Now men routinely speak about their tailor or their shoemaker. Men are at the stage now when they are comfortable buying jewelry for themselves. Look at friendship bracelets. Straight guys come back from a family holiday wearing four or five of them and are perfectly happy to keep them on in the office. It's not a great leap from a friendship bracelet to something more precious and permanent.'

With no little thanks to the advent of gay marriage, Fennell reports a growing demand for pavé-set diamond rings for men, such as his Spangle Rings in black or white diamonds. 'It's a terribly banal question to ask if a piece of jewelry is designed for a man or a woman when the only sensible answer is both,' he says.

www.theofennell.com

Opposite, top. 18ct white-gold Bee brooch set with black and white diamonds and blue sapphires.

Left and opposite, bottom. 18ct white-gold and pavé-diamond skull dress studs, and detail.

CHAPTER TWO

CUFFLINKS AND DRESS STUDS

—

CUFFLINKS AND DRESS STUDS

'Most charming and very original in design is the series of cufflinks given to the Tsar by his wife on the occasion of the christening of each of their five children.'

Alexander von Solodkoff, *The Jewel Album of Tsar Nicholas II* (1997)

The life story of Tsar Nicholas II, last emperor of Russia, is told in a hand-painted and annotated album of cufflinks, dress studs and stick pins now in the Kremlin Museum in Moscow. Between 1879 and 1914 the tsar lovingly recorded annual commemorative gifts from his extended Russian and European royal families, as well as jeweled mementos of his coronation, the tercentenary of the Romanov dynasty and the birth of his five children. The album depicts arguably the greatest collection of late nineteenth- and twentieth-century men's cufflinks ever amassed. The makers favoured by the imperial family included Fabergé, to whom Empress Alexandra would send designs, Cartier (patronized by the tsar's mother, Dowager Empress Maria Feodorovna) and Garrard, which British royal relatives favoured.

Although the French cuff (a soft turn-back 'kissing cuff') came into fashion in 1910, the tsar favoured the barrel cuff: a single starched cone joined by the jeweled link. His taste led fashion in Russia and Europe. The most popular design was the double-sided cufflink, a chain link joining a pair of cabochon gems set in yellow gold with a rose-cut diamond surround. Guilloché pearlescent enamel hearts, ovals and miniature imperial Easter eggs also feature prominently. The tsar also owned single-sided jeweled links with gold chain-and-bar fastenings, the bar often intricately figured and decorated with a ribbon of pavé diamonds. Less common were pivot links, a gem-set terminal with solid-gold bar and ball tail.

The album is poignant because the personal jewelry of the last tsar was lost during the Revolution that killed him and his family in 1918. But imperial jewels do surface on the auction market. At Sotheby's 'Romanov Heirlooms' sale in 2009, a pair of gold and enamel Lalique Bacchus cufflinks (see page 16) sold for £37,250 following a high estimate of £2,500, and a Vladimir Finikov gold cufflink set with a swirl of diamonds, cabochon rubies and cabochon sapphires realized £13,750 from a high estimate of £900.

The tsar's cufflinks and dress studs teach us to appreciate the quality and beauty of a jewel from every angle. If the object doesn't satisfy the eye when you turn it in the palm of your hand, it is a muggle. The first sign of a good link is the absence of a torpedo fastening, the very common T-bar

Page 56. The actor Riz Ahmed attends the Academy Awards in 2017 wearing a sapphire-blue Ermenegildo Zegna cocktail suit and classic mother-of-pearl dress studs.

Above. Vladimir Finikov gold cufflinks from about 1880, set with swirls of diamonds, cabochon sapphires and cabochon rubies.

Opposite. Tsar Nicholas II of Russia in about 1900, wearing his customary starched barrel cuffs.

Below. Imperial Russian cufflinks by Carl Fabergé (1909), pierced and engraved with double-headed eagles set with rose-cut diamonds.

'When stocking a collection of fine cufflinks, there must be one 'Switzerland': a design of neutral simplicity that works with jeans, tweeds or black tie.'

soldered to the underside of the terminal, that swivels on a central pivot. Contemporary collections by fine jewel houses invariably favour the practicality of a solid pivot link or the whale-back fastening with an articulated fishtail at the base that snaps 90 degrees to secure the cuff. These solid links are the easiest to fasten without the services of a butler. That said, the knack of threading a chain link or a chain and bar through four buttonholes takes very little practice, and the craft of chain-making is kept alive by artist jewelers.

When stocking a collection of fine cufflinks, there must be one 'Switzerland': a design of neutral simplicity that works with jeans, tweeds or black tie. In the 1970s Cartier produced Juste un Clou, a nail bent into a perfect circle. These links in yellow, white and pink gold – plain or embellished with diamonds – snap open with a miniature vanishing hinge and exemplify precious simplicity.

From the same period, Elsa Peretti designed for Tiffany & Co. a collection that is peerless in its casual simplicity. Her tactile silver Bean cufflink, made from ruthenium (a metal in the platinum family), has travelled well from the disco decade. Peretti was preceded in the 1950s and 1960s as guest artist at Tiffany & Co. by Jean Schlumberger. There are of course as many interpretations of the knot link cast in metal as there are ivory or bone cufflinks shaped like buttons. The great Schlumberger went further with the knot link, casting it in 18ct textured gold to create a clever *trompe l'œil*.

The writer Judith Price chose Paul Flato's solid 18ct-gold Nuts & Bolts cufflinks for the cover of her book *Masterpieces of American Jewelry* in 2004. The witty utility link that screws the cuff into place was in fact attributed to Fulco di Verdura, who produced designs for Flato in the 1930s. Nuts & Bolts is still a best-seller for the house of Verdura. David Yurman's Streamline translates the nut-and-bolt shape into a solid silver and 18ct yellow-gold link. The tradition of making utilitarian objects into fine jewelry has produced other modern classics, such as Solange Azagury-Partridge's Ball and Chain blackened 18ct yellow-gold chain-link wrecking balls.

It is the mark of a skilled fine jeweler to balance strength and delicacy in design. Take the married artist jewelry duo Gary Wright and Sheila Teague's 18ct yellow-gold Bee cufflinks (see page 244), for example. The insect is solid and heavy, set with a chain and bar. The body is smooth and the delicate tracery on its wings bears all the hallmarks of being handmade. You could put a piece of Wright & Teague yellow gold in the British Museum and it would be among friends. When Wright & Teague use gemstones for men's jewelry, the balance is perfect. The Celestial cufflink in yellow gold is an irregular, organic circular pool within which pavé-set diamonds float.

Yellow gold has experienced a revival for the first time since the much-maligned 1970s, when men's jewelry was last considered mainstream. That decade has been reassessed by a new generation of collectors, who are driving auction prices for the work of such jewelers as Andrew Grima ever upwards. His geometric design of textured yellow-gold squares from 1973 sold at Sotheby's in 2011 for £3,000 from a high estimate of £1,200.

The baton cufflink is one of the classics that every fine jeweler worth his or her salt will address. It comprises two tubular bars cinched by a solid metal handcuff device, and the design can be a fixed baton or sold with interchangeable bars, most commonly made from lapis lazuli, onyx and malachite, as well as yellow and white gold. A classic Van Cleef & Arpels yellow-gold fixed-baton link (see page 47) is mystery-set around the waist with a delicate ruby or sapphire band, and may be finished with matching cabochon stones on the finials.

Left. Wright & Teague's Spirit Stone 18ct textured yellow-gold cufflinks.

Opposite. Carré cufflinks in 18ct textured, stepped yellow gold by Grima (c.1975).

Below. The Romano-Egyptian 18ct yellow-gold Celestial cufflinks by Wright & Teague, pavé set with white diamonds.

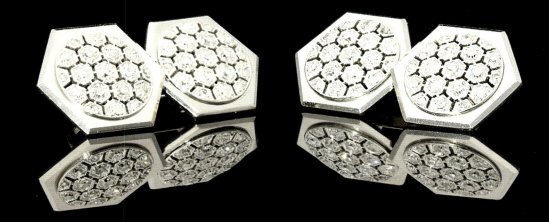

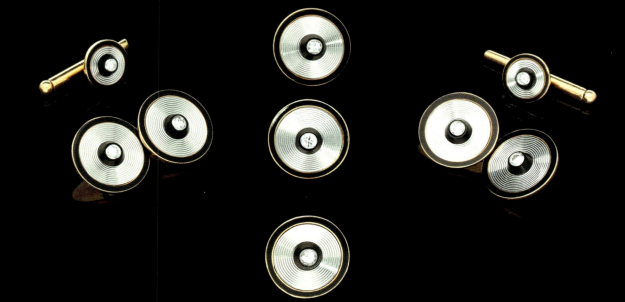

Boucheron's 'Quatre' collection (2004) led the way in breaking the rule about putting yellow and white gold in one design, and makes a virtue of mixing materials and finishes. Each baton in the Quatre link is a smooth chocolate ceramic, cinched with a thick girdle of double-ringed pink gold, smooth white gold and ridged yellow gold, plus a band of mosaic brown PVD. These links go with absolutely everything, from denim to grey flannel.

Jewelers who go beyond the classic cufflink designs are high-risk and high-reward. One of the most innovative modern designs is by Francesca Grima, who takes two large striped pillows of chalcedony set in yellow gold and bores a canal up, over and into the stones with a white-gold rivulet of diamonds (see page 60). Such a piece displays the bravura flamboyance of her father, Andrew. Theo Fennell has elevated the cufflink to sculpture in miniature. His white-gold frogs resting on yellow-gold lily pads are described with the precision of a zoologist (see page 52).

A gem-set novelty cufflink represents an opportunity for a fine jeweler to make magic. (When high jewelers talk about novelty cufflinks, they do not mean Union flags, emojis, Warhol's Marilyn or enamel eyeballs.) Novelty links with an important story to tell always resonate with collectors. The Burlington Arcade antique jeweler Hancocks owns a magnificent unsigned 1930s dress set (see page 66, top), with mystery-set sapphires set within three bars of diamonds with a circular diamond surround. According to the company's bespoke director, Guy Burton, the design was inspired by the steering wheel of a Bluebird V: the car in which Sir Malcolm Campbell broke his final land-speed record in 1935. Bentley & Skinner has a particular eye for novelty cufflinks with historic provenance, such as its yellow-gold and enamel Asprey playing cards, part of a special commission for the men implicated in the infamous Tranby Croft baccarat scandal of 1890.

The Mayfair antique jeweler, Cartier expert and British dealer for Verdura, Harry Fane, has bemoaned the fact that even the grandest dinners in private houses and palaces favour a smoking jacket worn with an open-necked shirt. One wonders whether this won't be the cue for smart men to wear dress studs in an open-necked Marcella shirt and save the smallest of sartorial treasures from extinction. Verdura's Night & Day dress set, made for Cole Porter, would look grand when worn in such dégagé fashion.

The most bewitching dress set this author saw bar none when writing *Jewelry for Gentlemen* was in the inventory of Lucas Rarities (see page 44). Made by Chaumet in 1925, the circular links and studs are set in 18ct white gold with three cushions of moonstone, interspersed with a three-pronged swish of European-cut diamonds, with a total carat weight of 3.3 in the set. The dress studs are unusually large – roughly the size of a British penny – and echo detachable buttons set in diamonds, marcasite or cut steel fashionable at the seventeenth-century court of Louis XIV at Versailles.

Cufflinks and dress studs continue to fascinate contemporary fine jewelers, who would not waste their energy if there weren't gentlemen who still wished to wear them. Outstanding new designs that are candidates for 'future antique' status include Jojo Grima's white-gold miniature cube links stacked at irregular levels and set with diamonds and sapphires, Shaun Leane's 18ct yellow-gold Eagle Skull links (see page 78), Stephen Webster's rhodium-plated silver Hammerhead shark links (see page 94) and David Yurman's space-age Meteorite cufflinks and dress studs set in sterling silver.

Above. Enamel and rose-cut-diamond playing-card cufflinks (c.1895) from Bentley & Skinner.

Opposite. An 18ct white-gold, moonstone and diamond dress stud by Chaumet. Courtesy of Lucas Rarities. Tailoring by Henry Poole & Co.

Below. Asprey gold-and-enamel baccarat playing-card cufflinks (c.1910). Courtesy of Bentley & Skinner.

Overleaf. Cartier cross-etched yellow-gold dice cufflinks set with round brilliant-cut diamonds (c.1955). Courtesy of Bentley & Skinner.

SHAUN LEANE

'There was always demand from men for my jewelry, but now the client is more confident, experimental and hungry for a refined aesthetic.'

Shaun Leane is one of the world's most influential contemporary jewelry designers, and a bellwether for the trade. So when in 2017 he produced his first dedicated men's jewelry collection since 2005, the industry took note. In the intervening years, Leane has moved from Hatton Garden to a showroom and workshop space in Woodstock Street, Mayfair, and in 2015 his twenty-two-year collaboration with his creative soulmate the late Alexander 'Lee' McQueen was celebrated with the Victoria and Albert Museum's exhibition 'Savage Beauty'. But above all, and not coincidentally, Leane has begun wearing his own jewelry.

'I have been in love with jewelry since I started my apprenticeship in Hatton Garden thirty-three years ago,' says Leane, 'but I wore very little of it. The first piece I made for myself was a cut-down set diamond eternity ring. I made one for me and one for Lee.' Today Leane wears his white-gold and diamond-set Talon earrings, his yellow-gold Serpent bracelet, a mourning ring dating from 1782 and numerous others, including a pavé-diamond white-gold Quill ring (see page 32) and his interlocking white-diamond Entwined stacking rings.

Like Andrew Grima, Leane is a sculptor of beautiful objects that romance stones with sinuous precious metalwork, rather than simply framing attention-stealing solitaires. He produces strong pieces with streamlined, sharp contours that appeal to men and women equally. 'Men are being a lot more daring now,' he says. 'There's a new confidence today.'

The men's collection of 2017 is made entirely in silver and eschews gemstones, although a diamond-set collection is in production. 'Everything I do has a point,' says Leane of the refined designs that include all the disciplines: cufflinks, tie slides, rings, bracelets, pendants, ear studs and lapel pins. 'It's time for the men's brooch,' he says. 'A beautiful piece of jewelry on the lapel of a jacket is a modern interpretation of wearing a flower in your buttonhole.' The tradition of sporting a fresh flower may survive now only when men wear morning dress for a wedding or race meeting. But it makes ostensibly feminine, floral jewels like Leane's Cherry Blossom look absolutely right in a man's lapel.

Delicate and refined as Leane's aesthetic might be, his work on the grand scale has the ability to seduce both sexes. His White Light brooch, which sold at Christie's in 2010 for $1.5 million, was a snowscape of white-gold and enamel branches cradling thirteen D-flawless Steinmetz princess-cut diamonds. The black swan to White Light, the spiky circular Thistle brooch entrapping large black Tahitian pearls (overleaf), was made in 2006 as a pair for Sarah Jessica Parker and McQueen to wear at the AngloMania' Met Gala in New York.

Opposite. Shaun Leane, photographed by Ian Winstanley, wearing his Beetle brooch, Serpent bracelet and white-gold and diamond Quill ring.

Overleaf. The Tahitian pearl Thistle brooch made for Alexander McQueen, as worn at the 'AngloMania: Tradition and Transgression in British Fashion' Met Gala in New York in 2006.

Right. The gold-plated Arc cufflinks from Shaun Leane's men's collection of 2017.

Opposite, top. The 18ct yellow-gold Heavy Serpent bracelet is articulated to coil sinuously around the wrist.

Opposite, bottom. 18ct yellow-gold Eagle Skull cufflinks.

The Thistle brooch is emblematic of the synergy between fashion and jewelry that McQueen and Leane forged for more than two decades. Leane says of McQueen that 'he changed the silhouette of fashion, and we worked brilliantly together because we were really good friends.' Both young men had served formal apprenticeships in their respective fields: McQueen as a Savile Row bespoke tailor and Leane as a maker of fine jewelry in Hatton Garden. They had been friends for three years before Leane invited McQueen to visit him at his workplace, English Traditional Jewellery in east London.

Leane spent thirteen years doing bench work there, setting estate jewelry that supplied Bond Street's grand old houses with parures that could have been made in 1885, not 1995. 'If it wasn't for Lee [McQueen], I would still be sitting in a little workshop making tiaras,' he says. 'Instead, I became the Jekyll and Hyde of jewelry. He was blown away by the craft and the detail and the intricacy of what I was

creating. I think it kind of sank into his mind and he then asked me to make jewelry for his shows.'

By day Leane was handling aristocratic family jewels at English Traditional Jewellery. By night and at the weekends he and McQueen would dream up jewelry reminiscent of body armour, such as the aluminium Coiled corset displayed in McQueen's Autumn/Winter 1999 catwalk show, 'The Overlooked'. McQueen's Spring/Summer 1996 show, 'The Hunger', was the occasion of the debut of Leane's Tusk earring, which has become inextricably linked with the house of Shaun Leane. Of McQueen, Leane said at the launch of 'Savage Beauty' that 'he was part of my bones and my blood, so when he passed [in 2010] I couldn't not continue to create and not further that energy.'

'I like to fuse elements of traditional with a contemporary design approach,' says Leane. 'We cannot look to the future of design without remembering our past.' Nowhere was his knowledge of historical

'We cannot look to the future of design without remembering our past.'

jewelry design techniques tested more than in the creation of Contra Mundum, a majestic, fairy-tale white-gold and diamond chain-mail evening glove made in 2011 for his patron and friend the fashion muse Daphne Guinness. The glove is constructed from 1,000 grams of gold chain link as supple as chiffon, and armoured with a hand-engraved white-gold cuff, rings, claws and bird motifs pavé set with more than 5,000 white diamonds.

Leane is equally passionate about bespoke commissions that interpret some of the most private emotions within a small, discreet piece of jewelry. In 2015 he created a pair of platinum seal rings inlaid with bicolour agate hand-engraved with a moth motif. The inner sleeve of the ring was sterling silver. 'The rings were made for a man who had tragically lost his son at a very young age,' he explains. 'Every element of the design, including an engraving inside the ring, represented the young man. I think that was one of the most moving experiences for me as a jeweler.'

www.shaunleane.com

Opposite, top. A yellow-gold vermeil and diamond Tusk bracelet.

Opposite, bottom. The 18ct yellow-gold Sabre pendant and Beetle brooch. Tailoring by Sir Tom Baker.

Below. The 22ct yellow-gold Beetle brooch exhibited in 2014 at SHOWstudio's SHOWcabinet project, personally worn by Shaun Leane.

SOLANGE AZAGURY-PARTRIDGE

'I have never designed jewelry to be merely pretty.
It's a waste of an opportunity.'

Solange-Azagury Partridge's instinctive talent for disrupting traditional jewelry design first emerged in 1987, when she designed her own engagement ring. The sinuous silver bombé set with a rough diamond chip was worlds from the usual prim sparkling white-diamond solitaire. She saw the beauty in included, unpolished stones, anticipating De Beers' celebrated rough-diamond 'Talisman' collection by about twenty years. Azagury-Partridge's 'cool Britannia' approach to fine jewelry allowed her to leap from a Westbourne Grove atelier that locals mistook for a bordello to the Place Vendôme in Paris when Gucci Group's Tom Ford personally chose her to design *haute joaillerie* for Boucheron in 2001.

'Alpha' – Azagury-Partridge's first men's collection, designed in 2014 – was characteristically provocative. Its uniting factor was her use of sandblasted yellow gold blackened with rhodium so that it slowly reveals its gleam with time and touch. The collection is a dark storm of talismanic themes, black humour and ancient symbolism, men's jewelry with *cojones*: dirty gold Ball and Chain cufflinks, stallion Stud earrings, the Tied-Up bangle, reminiscent of barbed wire, and the Family Jewels pendant, comprising well-placed hand grenades on either side of a phallic bullet. A viper's-head ring with emerald eyes, sharp fangs and an articulated jaw is a thing of dark beauty, as is the Samson

bracelet, handwoven with blackened gold chains and a lock of one's lover's hair. Stones are used sparingly and with minimum sparkle, hence Azagury-Partridge's use of her beloved misty cabochon emeralds for the Villain ring and pendant, set in blackened human bone motifs.

These bits of rough with dark exteriors that reveal a heart of gold describe the Azagury-Partridge man. 'Men always bought my jewelry,' says Azagury-Partridge, 'but until [GQ editor] Dylan [Jones] suggested that I get involved in London Collections: Men, I hadn't put a dedicated men's collection out there. Men can get it very wrong with jewelry. Some don't pull it off and that makes me quite queasy. So I suppose I wanted to design men's jewelry that didn't make me ill.'

'Alpha' was designed with an eye to the way Azagury-Partridge's model son Otis wears her jewelry. 'I can't quite believe how much jewelry Otis wears, but he wears it so well,' she says. 'He will wear my bone ear studs, emerald Villain pendant, rings on both hands and bracelets on both wrists.'

'Alpha' is a gritty, urban collection that doesn't immediately draw attention to itself, and that is why men tend not to feel threatened by it. It represents design by stealth, with coded messages that reveal themselves only on closer inspection. It is characteristic of Azagury-Partridge's wry sense of humour to take the concept of men's jewelry as something that can

Opposite. The 18ct blackened yellow-gold and cabochon-emerald Villain pendant. Tailoring by Sir Tom Baker.

Overleaf, clockwise from left. The pavé-set diamond Mirror Ball pendant in blackened 18ct white gold, worn in the lapel of a Sir Tom Baker city suit; the 18ct blackened yellow-gold Viper ring with cabochon-ruby eyes and articulated jaw; the 18ct blackened yellow-gold Love Knot bangle.

'You don't know how you will feel about a piece until you hold it in your hand.'

Opposite, top. The handwoven 18ct blackened yellow-gold chain-mail Samson bracelet is entwined with a lock of hair.

Opposite, bottom. The 18ct blackened yellow-gold and diamond Snake bangle.

Below. Solange Azagury-Partridge's Hotlips ring in 18ct blackened white gold set with round brilliant-cut diamonds. The red enamel version of Hotlips is in the permanent collection of the Victoria and Albert Museum.

intimidate and give that energy to the wearer. This is pugnacious jewelry at its most powerful: a balled fist Bareknuckle pendant (see page 228), the Dark Lord knuckleduster ring and a writhing, coiled Snake bangle with icy diamond eyes. The Muz knuckleduster – a blackened-gold beast with concave face and two square-cut stones sunk into either side of the shank – is a heavyweight diamond geezer.

By concealing the shine of the yellow gold in 'Alpha', Azagury-Partridge has effectively toughened and aged her men's jewelry. When I revisit her Lionheart ring at her by-appointment atelier in Paddington, London, in 2017, having encountered it first in 2014 at the former flagship on Carlos Place in Mayfair, I find that time has already revealed streaks of yellow gold in the mane where the blackening has worn away. The seams of

gleam accentuate the heart-shaped ruby in the lion's forehead and his diamond eyes.

'Jewelry is very tactile,' says Azagury-Partridge. 'I suppose you don't know how you will feel about a piece until you hold it in your hand.' Having tried on several pieces from the 'Alpha' collection, I can attest that the weight is substantial enough for the wearer to appreciate the preciousness of the metal, but the balance of the design makes these pieces feel as easy to wear as a T-shirt. There isn't that consciousness of wearing jewelry, not least because 'Alpha' is designed for a modern, urban gent, not a peacock dandy.

Azagury-Partridge cut her teeth at Butler & Wilson, then London's most outrageous costume jeweler, with a clientele of club kids, pop stars and drag queens, then learned about the great jewelry marques through handling antique

Cartier, Van Cleef & Arpels, Chaumet and Boucheron masterpieces while working for Gordon Watson. The marriage of the two – the exuberance of costume and the craftsmanship of the great houses – was her starting point.

Although distinct themes emerge in Azagury-Partridge's work – among them geometry, Pop art, articulation and the natural world – the only uniting factor between, say, the sculptural enamel Hotlips ring, as plump as Dalí's Mae West sofa, and the tasselled diamond fringe ring that cascades chains of pavé-set stones around the finger is that they've sprung from the same extraordinary mind. Both the Musée des Arts Décoratifs in Paris and London's Victoria and Albert Museum have chosen iconic pieces for their permanent collections.

There's a paradoxical quality to high jewelry that shows a complete absence of self-importance. As Azagury-Partridge says, 'I think jewelry is such a luxury and

so costly, it should bring you pleasure and joy.' There is an affinity between her precious but playful Smarties, cartoon bugs and bees, disco balls and pouting lips and the great Jean Schlumberger's Bird on a Rock brooch, a whimsical bejeweled bird perched on top of the 128.54ct yellow Tiffany diamond. Like Schlumberger, Azagury-Partridge treats serious stones with a very light touch.

It is the mark of exceptional jewelry design that an idea such as Quatre can be forever revisited with combinations of differently coloured gold, stones and finishes. Hotlips is a prime example of how the character of the shape is transformed when it is made in scarlet enamel, pavé-set rubies or yellow gold. Azagury-Partridge keeps adding pieces to 'Alpha' as the dialogue between her designs for men and for women becomes ever more fluent.

www.solange.co.uk

Above, left. The 18ct blackened yellow-gold Bone ring.

Above, right. The diamond and 18ct blackened yellow-gold Snake ring.

Opposite. The 18ct blackened yellow-gold W.M.D. A.K.A. Family Jewels pendant.

'I think jewelry is such a luxury and so costly,
it should bring you pleasure and joy.'

STEPHEN WEBSTER

'The client for men's fine jewelry is there. He is not necessarily blinging and may only wear one or two pieces of Stephen Webster at a time, but he's collecting like the watch guys.'

In the summer of 2017 Harrods unveiled its first men's fine jewelry room dedicated to a single brand, on the subterranean men's fashion floor. The name chosen to meet the anticipated demand for exceptional pieces of men's jewelry was Stephen Webster. In the twenty years since he designed his seminal men's collection, 'Rayman', Webster has consistently proved that men will follow where he leads: 'through stubbornness and perhaps naïvety I have made it my mission to provide a product that lies between the provocative and the wearable.'

The man who has often been compared visually with Bob Dylan, Keith Richards and Johnny Depp's Cap'n Jack Sparrow is the black diamond of British jewelers. Designs that appear rock 'n' roll, gothic or biker from a distance reveal themselves as rich and complex. Take his best-loved and shamelessly imitated collection, 'Crystal Haze', which submerges coloured gemstones beneath quartz. The effect on a men's white-gold cufflink with red garnet beneath a faceted dome of clear quartz surrounded by pavé-set white diamonds adds depth and mystery that make the piece more masculine than a solitaire gemstone.

There is wit and intelligence as well as strength in Webster's jewelry, such as the white-gold Shark Jaw ring that bites the finger between two rows of white diamond-set teeth, or a sinuous Rayman rhodium-plated crucifix inlaid with black sapphires. When he first emerged on the London jewelry scene under his own name, in the early 1990s, Webster's work was compared to Chrome Hearts. Expectations were adjusted in 2000, when Madonna and Guy Ritchie exchanged Webster wedding bands and Stephen Webster was christened 'Lord of the Rings'.

Speaking from his office above the Mayfair flagship of Garrard, where he has been creative director since 2008 and is currently a chairman, Webster contemplates the man who is in the market for a rose-gold Figaro-link England Made Me bracelet with rose-gold and black-diamond Churchill clasp for £25,000. 'A guy in Harrods spent £300,000 on three belts made with precious metal buckles and exotic skins, so I don't think price is the issue. Presentation is,' he says. 'The opportunity to present a pure men's world of jewelry in an environment designed to put guys at ease is one I've been talking about for a couple of years.'

Webster points to the extraordinary yellow-gold, diamond and ruby Japanese Warrior Mask ring that he designed and made himself, a gift from his wife, Anastasia, who has worked tirelessly to build the Stephen Webster brand. 'That ring hasn't stopped getting attention for twenty years, but I can't always walk round

Opposite. Stephen Webster wears his Japanese Warrior Mask ring and England Made Me Cuban ceramic bracelet with gem-set England Made Me Revolutionary clasp.

Overleaf. The 18ct white-gold and diamond filigree Fly by Night pavé brooch. Tailoring by Sir Tom Baker.

Above. The 18ct white-gold, black and white rhodium-plated Shark Jaw ring, pavé set with white diamonds.

Opposite. Sterling silver Hammerhead tie pin and cufflinks, set with sapphires, from Stephen Webster's 'Jewels Verne' collection.

Below. The 18ct white-gold and black rhodium-plated Langoustine brooch pavé set with onyx, blue sapphires and black, silver and white diamonds.

being my own point of sale. The timing is right for a 100 per cent men's jewelry boutique in the men's department at Harrods.'

In addition to Harrods, Webster has a salon at London's most fashionable address, Mount Street, and a flagship on Rodeo Drive in Los Angeles, the spiritual home of his aesthetic. He is that rare talent that the film and music industries are prepared to pay for, rather than the usual awards-ceremony arrangement whereby the jewel houses pay big bucks to place their product on the red carpet.

'We've never been a particularly feminine brand,' says Webster when asked about his appeal for both sexes. 'If you come to LA, no way does that store look like a conventional women's jewelry shop. Men are comfortable coming into our store on Rodeo Drive. There are pieces I have made for women that I think would look really cool on a guy. I sold a pair of Hammerhead shark brooches with articulated fins to a woman that would look amazing on a man's lapel. It is definitely time to take men's jewelry to the next level.'

Webster's bench training and knowledge of jewelry have produced a bracelet collection that echoes the ingenuity of late Victorian jewels that divide to make multitasking pieces.

The 'England Made Me' collection presents a Figaro-link bracelet in matt or gloss black ceramic with interchangeable clasps inspired by the shape of a cigar cutter. Each plaque is crafted in an intriguing combination of materials, such as rose gold inlaid with red enamel and black diamonds. The plaques begin at £9,000, rendering 'England Made Me' an attractive proposition for the collector who wants several pieces of jewelry in one.

When asked about the men who get his jewelry, Webster riffs on the evolution of street style and the Autumn/Winter 2017 catwalk collaboration in Paris between Louis Vuitton and the cult skate/hip-hop brand Supreme. 'Street brands are moving way beyond the street,' he says. 'If a guy is dressed in any way not conventional for the business he is in, he's chosen to do that and to show you he's not just another suit. I think these are the guys who appreciate my jewelry. They aren't likely to wear more than one ring, a tie slide or a bracelet, but that's all it takes.'

'I've been in jewelry for a long time,' Webster says. 'In the early days there was a lot of uncertainty about whether men could get away with wearing bracelets, pendants and earrings. My early work was more geared towards the guy who was a weekend rock and roller. . .as well as the real rock and rollers who picked up on what I was doing. Selling to that crowd was quite easy, but rock-star jewelry isn't for everyone. A turning point came when David Beckham was photographed wearing pieces from my "Rayman" collection. That sent out a strong message.'

In the run-up to the Harrods opening, Webster reassessed his archive of designs for men and chose pieces from every collection to go into the new space: black sapphire and tsavorite Rayman cufflinks, a rhodium-plated silver oval Thorn bracelet, a yellow-gold and mother-of-pearl England Made Me switchblade pendant and the Beasts of London rings and links, inspired by the city's emblematic animals the leopard, eel, grasshopper, lion and Embankment fish. Seen together for the first time at Harrods, the work from Webster's two decades of design for men demonstrates admirably why he is one of the most directional jewelers in the business today.

www.stephenwebster.com

Above. The 18ct rose-gold, black-sapphire and ruby England Made Me Revolutionary clasp is made to be worn with Webster's Cuban ceramic bracelets.

Opposite. The 14ct yellow-gold Queen's Walk ring, set with black-onyx inlay and oxblood ceramic, from Webster's men's collection 'Thames' of 2017, designed in collaboration with the skater-artist Blondey McCoy.

CHAPTER THREE

STICK PINS, STUDS AND SLIDES

—

STICK PINS, STUDS AND SLIDES

The story of the William III diamond epitomizes the glory of jeweled masterpieces in miniature. The stick pin entered the gentleman's wardrobe in the late eighteenth century, when the Prince Regent's sartorial Svengali George 'Beau' Brummell popularized the pristine white-linen stock that consigned the tiered lace cravat to history. The Regency dandy wore his dark tailcoat and waistcoat with a dramatically high, round break framing the stock, with the pin prominently displayed.

The stick pin's demise is a consequence of practicality. Where once the pin, however decorative, served the purpose of holding the stock in place, now a chap isn't going to spend north of £140 on a 7-twill Hermès silk tie only to pit it with more holes than Caesar's corpse. Thus the stick pin has migrated to the lapel, where it has become something of a fashion on red carpets worldwide.

The migration from cravat to lapel has allowed peacock males who collect pins to include jeweled jabot pins, which were fashionable among Edwardians and reached a peak of flamboyance in the art deco era. Whereas a stick pin rarely has more than a neat little gold plug mechanism to sheath the spike, a jabot pin will have a highly decorative, jeweled stopper that is designed to be displayed.

One of the most sublime jabot pins, the Lotus Flower, was made by Cartier in 1917. Two large carved emeralds are set in platinum and white diamonds with a diamond horseshoe curving down around the platinum pin, which has a finial encrusted with diamonds and emeralds. But compared to the jabot, the stick pin is an undemanding piece of jewelry: spike it into and out of the lapel and forget about it. The jewel is infinitely less work than a wilting boutonnière, and tests the creativity of design and setting on a surface smaller than a fivepenny piece.

'Stick pins are a microcosm of jewelry design,' Wartski's managing director, Geoffrey Munn, told the *Financial Times* in 2016. Most famous jewelry marques did make tie pins, but prices have risen much more modestly than those of jewelry signed by an important name, meaning that good pieces can be had for more reasonable sums.

Page 98. The actor Jon Hamm wears a sterling silver tie slide by Tom Ford at the designer's Fall 2016 fashion show in New York.

Above. A late nineteenth-century Fabergé yellow-gold stick pin in the form of a coiled snake suspending a miniature egg in translucent red enamel with guilloché ground.

Opposite. The English politician and dandy Sir Philip Sassoon (c.1920) wearing an immaculate natural-pearl cravat pin. His extensive accounts with Cartier London suggest that the piece is signed by the French jewel house.

Left. Tiffany & Co. large emerald briolette grasped by two tightly entwined diamond-set snakes to a gold stick pin, c.1900.

Only houses, such as Cartier, that produce 100-piece high-jewelry collections every year have the luxury of being able to create extravagant novelties of this kind. In 2009, at the centenary party for Cartier's Fifth Avenue mansion in New York, Justin Timberlake was photographed wearing a diamond and onyx Panthère stick pin with emerald eyes in his tie. Pierre Rainero, the house's director of image, style and heritage, told the author in 2017 that designs for a Panthère de Cartier lapel pin inspired by an archive acquisition from the 1920s were in the early stages of development.

With the exception of Theo Fennell, who has fashioned one of his yellow-and-white-gold Bee Different insects with a green tourmaline body into a handsome stick pin (see page 48), contemporary jewelers still omit stick pins from their collections, so the search is largely restricted to antiques dealers and auction houses. There is a finite number of top-class antique pins by the major marques and, as the vogue for lapel pins gathers momentum, prices will inevitably rise. The auction market is already reflecting this interest, with sinuous, figurative art nouveau enamel old masters by the French artist jeweler René Lalique leading the field. Two gold, enamel and glass Lalique stick pins – Swans and Female in Profile – sold at Sotheby's New York in 2016 for $35,000.

Opposite. A Russian imperial yellow-gold double-headed-eagle stick pin by Fabergé, surmounted with a crown and set with a ruby (c.1910). Courtesy of Wartski. Tailoring by Turnbull & Asser.

Below. An oval ruby and old brilliant-cut diamond set in silver on a twisted yellow-gold stick pin (c.1890) from Bentley & Skinner.

'With the exception of Theo Fennell, who has fashioned one of his yellow-and-white-gold Bee Different insects with a blue topaz body into a handsome stick pin, contemporary jewelers still omit stick pins from their collections, so the search is largely restricted to antiques dealers and auction houses.'

Above. This early twentieth-century oval peridot stick pin, millegrain-set with rose-cut diamonds, was sold by Sotheby's London in 2017 for £3,500.

Opposite. A late Victorian ruby and seed-pearl 18ct rose-gold stick pin from the author's collection.

The perceived impracticality of stick pins held prices down at first, and led auction houses to group pieces rather than sell them as single lots. Thirty-two gem-set stick pins from the Christian, Lady Hesketh estate sale at Sotheby's Geneva in 2007 realized 27,600CHF on a high estimate of 15,000CHF. But in 2012 a single natural-pearl stick pin set in white gold and dated 1915 sold at Sotheby's New York for $40,625, from a high estimate of $20,000, and in 2017 a magnificent early twentieth-century oval peridot stick pin surrounded by a three-tier openwork frame of millegrain-set rose-cut diamonds sold at Sotheby's London for £3,500.

In 2016 a serpent design in bloodstone and yellow gold for an unsigned stick pin was estimated by Sotheby's at £120–80. It sold for £2,000 because the snake was the Cavendish family emblem and the sale was titled 'Deborah Duchess of Devonshire: The Last of the Mitford Sisters'. One of Munn's appearances on the BBC's *Antiques Roadshow* in 2012 unearthed a Fabergé two-colours-gold-and-sapphire imperial eagle stick pin valued at £10,000, one of many liberally handed out on Tsar Nicholas II's visit to Sandringham in 1893 to ask for the hand of Queen Victoria's granddaughter Princess Alix of Hesse.

As the tsar's jewel album demonstrates, stick pins were a fashionable gift to present to members of royal households. To call them mass-produced would be churlish, but even if it is by Fabergé, a presentation pin will not touch the price of a pin personally owned by a member of the imperial family. In 2008 Christie's sold a Friedrich Köchli MM monogram yellow-gold stick pin surmounted by a rose-cut diamond and cabochon-ruby imperial crown for £3,750. The presentation piece was commissioned by Grand Duke Michael Mikhailovich.

Between them, Bentley & Skinner and Wartski corner the market in London for exceptional stick pins. The sales director of the former, Omar Vaja, is a passionate advocate of the stick pin worn in the lapel button, while Wartski's Thomas Holman has made a study of stick pins and substantially bolstered the inventory at Wartski. Bentley & Skinner has a particularly strong collection of Golden Age stick pins from the second half of the nineteenth century, such as a LaCloche Frères art deco purple pate de verre carved Buddha with a diamond headdress and a fleur-de-lys

'When you go shopping for stick pins, the piece will inevitably choose you rather than vice versa. Jeweled pins were made to reflect a predilection for gambling, the turf, theatre, aviation and the male and female form, to name a few favourites.'

finial, dated *c.*1920 and set in platinum. The most seductive piece is a coiled gold snake holding a red enamelled egg between its fangs, made in Russian art nouveau style (see page 100). Animal pieces collected by Bentley & Skinner are the liveliest examples of capturing the beast's character, such as a yellow-gold fox's head from the 1890s with beady rose-cut diamond eyes.

Of course, Wartski has a blaze of Fabergé stick pins that would romance any lapel day or night, but the pin that catches and holds the eye is a textured gold circle reminiscent of a gold nugget embedded with a diamond, a ruby and a sapphire, made in 1895 by the US jewelry giant Bailey Banks & Biddle. On a purely practical level, such a jewel can accommodate practically any cloth it is put against, from Harris tweed to the finest black barathea.

When you go shopping for stick pins, the piece will inevitably choose you rather than vice versa. Jeweled pins were made to reflect a predilection for gambling, the turf, theatre, aviation and the male and female form, to name a few favourites. Late Victorian cameo and intaglio stick pins depicting the Roman emperor Hadrian's lover Antinous were popular, and in the language of jewelry those and stick pins featuring St Sebastian were discreet ways to advertise an inclination for men. It is intriguing to think of the belle époque stick pin as a precursor to Grindr.

The tie stud is basically a pierced earring setting that penetrates the tie silk and is secured into a metal plug that locks the spike inside. The visible jewel is roughly the size of a pea. A chain and T-bar threads through the second button down on the shirt, ensuring that the tie doesn't slip sideways. Dandies will lift the tie with its perfect four-in-hand knot dimple before securing the tie stud, giving it a wave that looks rather dashing.

Sad to report that very few jewelers make tie studs today because, quite frankly, very few men wear them. What might look like a black- or white-pearl tie stud in a Victorian or Edwardian photograph is in fact a stick pin, because the stud mechanism didn't come into fashion until after the Second World War and didn't last much beyond the 1970s – hence the fact that so few antique tie studs of quality were made or have subsequently come to auction. Natural-pearl studs are exceptionally rare, and many tie-tack designs are on the naff register of novelty jewelry.

Above. A sapphire-and-diamond flower stick pin sold by Tiffany & Co. in about 1950.

Opposite. An art deco platinum-mounted LaCloche Frères Buddha stick pin (c.1920) from Bentley & Skinner, carved from purple *pâte de verre* and embellished with a rose-cut diamond halo and fleur-de-lys base. Tailoring by Turnbull & Asser.

'The tie stud is basically a pierced earring setting that penetrates the tie silk and is secured into a metal plug that locks the spike inside. The visible jewel is roughly the size of a pea.'

However, the revived interest in jewels for gentlemen has led such jewelers as Shaun Leane to revisit the tie stud. While we were shooting the pictures for *Jewelry for Gentlemen*, Leane proposed his yellow-gold and diamond feather earring to be set as a tie stud. Because earring mechanisms fit the tie-stud plug, he also experimented with 0.50ct solitaire-diamond tie studs and a trio of his yellow-gold vermeil Cherry Blossom studs with diamond centres to ornament a tie. Theo Fennell has allowed his yellow-gold and black-enamel bee to alight on the tie as an amusing precious stud.

The tie stud will not return as a key element of the well-dressed gentleman's jewelry wardrobe unless the proposal is made by trusted jewel houses. By contrast, the tie slide or tie bar, which clips the tie to the shirt placket, has made the most remarkable comeback since its heyday in the 1950s and 1960s, thanks to a combination of influences. The highly stylized cigarettes-and-chauvinism television series *Mad Men* (2007–15),

'The tie slide has become the Hollywood stylists' go-to sliver of precious metal to sharpen a red-carpet suit. ... Like the tie tack, the slide had too narrow a window in men's fashion after the Second World War to have built up much of an inventory of collectible designs.'

set in New York's advertising agency shark pool in the early 1960s, was practically an advertisement for the gold collar bar and the tie slide.

The tie slide has become the Hollywood stylists' go-to sliver of precious metal to sharpen a red-carpet suit. Tom Hiddleston, Ryan Gosling, Zac Efron, Liam Hemsworth, Austin Butler, Tom Hardy and Matthew McConaughey have all worn variations on the theme, but invariably made by fashion rather than jewel houses. Louis Vuitton, Tom Ford and Saint Laurent all produce simple sterling silver tie slides available for the low hundreds, which is really too close to bijoux for the big beasts of fine jewelry to countenance.

Like the tie tack, the slide had too narrow a window in men's fashion after the Second World War to have built up much of an inventory of collectible designs. An exception is Cartier's 14ct yellow-gold golf clubs, and knotted gold designs by Schlumberger for Tiffany & Co., Van Cleef & Arpels and Boucheron. Contemporary designers who always push tie-slide design beyond banality are Stephen Webster, David Yurman and Shaun Leane.

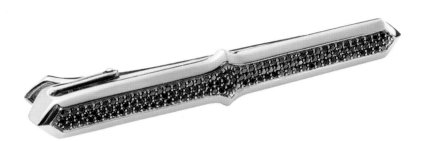

Left. Sterling silver and black-sapphire Rayman tie slide by Stephen Webster.

Opposite. The actor Tom Hardy attends the London premiere of *Dunkirk* in 2017, tailored by Gucci and wearing a distinctive antique yellow-gold tie slide set with rubies and diamonds.

BOUCHERON

'An up-and-coming jeweler, Frédéric Boucheron, came to the auction hoping to buy the Grand Mazarin ... His firm, established only twenty-four years earlier, already was a significant rival to older firms by virtue of its superior craftsmanship and innovative technology.'

Penny Proddow and Marion Fasel, *Diamonds: A Century of Spectacular Jewels* **(1996)**

In 1887 diamonds belonging to the French royal family were auctioned in what was christened 'the sale of the century'. Stones that had once belonged to King Louis XIV, Empress Joséphine and France's last empress, Eugénie, brought the world's jewel houses to Paris. Tiffany & Co. bought more than a third of the collection, but it was Frédéric Boucheron who carried off the prize 18.5ct Grand Mazarin diamond, bequeathed to Louis XIV in 1661. Boucheron set the gem in a ring for his wife.

Boucheron has perhaps the most romantic biography of all the Parisian high jewelers. Frédéric Boucheron opened his first shop in the arcades that flank the Palais Royal in 1858, at the height of the Second Empire, and was the first high jeweler to open on the Place Vendôme, in 1893. When César Ritz opened his eponymous hotel there in 1898, he and Boucheron became great friends and shared a glamorous clientele, including Prince Felix Yusupov, tsars Alexander III and Nicholas II of Russia and John Jacob Astor IV, who went down with *Titanic* in 1912 along with fabulous Boucheron jewels belonging to his wife, Madeleine.

According to Boucheron's website, 'Frédéric Boucheron was fascinated by gemstones,' but it was the quality, craftsmanship and ingenuity of the settings of the jewelry that made the house exceptional. It was one of the first jewelers to use the peacock-feather motif for diamond brooches, in the 1870s. In the 1880s it made intricate Renaissance Revival pendants, and in the 1890s its chief diamond-cutter initiated the fashion for engraving diamonds, such as a diamond-and-ruby bee brooch with engraved wafer-thin diamond wings, dating from about 1894.

Boucheron was an early exponent of art nouveau jewelry: it displayed the emerald-and-diamond Chestnut Leaf necklace at the World's Fair in Paris in 1900, and was also one of the first fine jewelers to sell the work of the art nouveau master René Lalique. House legend has it that Grand Duke Vladimir of Russia brought a scarf dropped at a ball by his future wife, Maria Pavlovna, to Frédéric Boucheron, and asked him to render the keepsake in gold. Weaving precious metal to mimic the suppleness of silk became a house style, as did the open-ended Question Mark necklace and Scarf necklaces such as the ruby, emerald, diamond and onyx design shown at the Exposition des Arts Décoratifs in Paris in 1925. This ingenious jewel divides to create a pair of bracelets and a choker.

Following Frédéric Boucheron's death in 1902, the business was directed by his son Louis. It was on Louis's watch that the most important order in the Place Vendôme's

A Boucheron cufflink case with interchangeable baton settings in 18ct yellow gold, 18ct white gold, rock crystal, lapis lazuli, onyx, malachite and leopard wood.

'Boucheron's Arctic brooch is a masterpiece: a benign polar bear described in white diamonds and sapphires pads across ice made from a slice of rock crystal surrounded by diamonds and set in white gold.'

history was placed, by the Maharaja of Patiala in 1928. The maharaja appeared at the door of no. 26 escorted by servants carrying six boxes full of precious stones – 7,571 diamonds and 1,432 emeralds alone – from which Boucheron set a suite of 149 pieces of jewelry for the maharaja. Boucheron's royal connections were furthered in 1930, when the Shah of Iran commanded Louis Boucheron to come to Tehran and inventory the imperial treasures. Boucheron was later appointed Official Curator and Guardian of the Iranian crown jewels.

Boucheron's art deco to mid-century jewelry lends itself to the male collector, particularly such designs of the 1930s as a magnificent diamond feather brooch (c.1939) that Sotheby's New York sold for

$137,000, from a high estimate of $50,000. In 2015 Sotheby's sold a substantial square-and-oval-link 18ct yellow-gold Boucheron bracelet dating from 1945 for £13,750, from a high estimate of £4,500. The yellow-gold stirrup cufflink design was a favourite Boucheron piece in the twentieth century, and is most collectible when made from twists of 18ct yellow gold or solid arches set with rubies or sapphires and matching cabochon stones in the terminals.

The serpent has been entwined with Boucheron's history since 1888, when Frédéric gave a talismanic snake necklace to his wife, Gabrielle, on the eve of his travels. The Boucheron snake appears at the turn of the twentieth century as a yellow-gold cravat ring and repeatedly

A 12.4ct rock crystal set in 18ct white gold is framed by pavé diamonds and surmounted by a diamond-and-sapphire polar bear in the Arctic brooch by Boucheron.

Above. Gold and lapis lazuli pyramid cufflinks by Boucheron (c.1935) set with circular brilliant-cut diamonds.

Below, left. Stirrup cufflinks by Boucheron with eight rectangular step-cut sapphires channel-set in 18ct yellow gold (c.1935).

Below, right. Boucheron heavy chain stirrup cufflinks (c.1920).

Overleaf, left. Diamond-and-sapphire art deco bar brooch by Boucheron, courtesy of Harry Fane. Tailoring by Sir Tom Baker.

Overleaf, right. Two wedding bands by Boucheron: the Quatre ring in 18ct white gold, black PVD and pavé diamonds; and an 18ct yellow-gold and brown-PVD ring.

in a striking yellow-gold stick pin in the form of a cobra. The present 'Serpent Bohème' collection doesn't offer a huge amount of crossover for male clients, although pink-gold bracelets and pendants set with black onyx do appeal. Arguably the most successful of Boucheron's contemporary collections was Quatre, designed by Solange Azagury-Partridge, who became creative director in 2001.

Quatre is an ingenious mash-up of precious materials that stack to form a collection of rings that have been a mammoth success with male clients. White, yellow and pink gold is combined with bands of white diamonds and mosaics of black PVD that unite in a seemingly endless choice of configurations. Boucheron has been famed for its animals since the actress Sarah Bernhardt asked Frédéric to

create replicas of her dogs, cats and birds for a series of rings and necklaces. The contemporary 'Animals' collection is not directed towards men, but poses fascinating propositions for men's right-hand rings, pins and pendants.

Boucheron's Arctic brooch is a masterpiece: a benign polar bear described in white diamonds and sapphires pads across ice made from a slice of rock crystal surrounded by diamonds and set in white gold. The black swan pendant Cypris is an exotic creature made from black sapphires, diamonds, rubies and blackened gold, with its neck looped around a white-gold chain. The rings display all the exuberance and ingenuity of the house.

www.boucheron.com

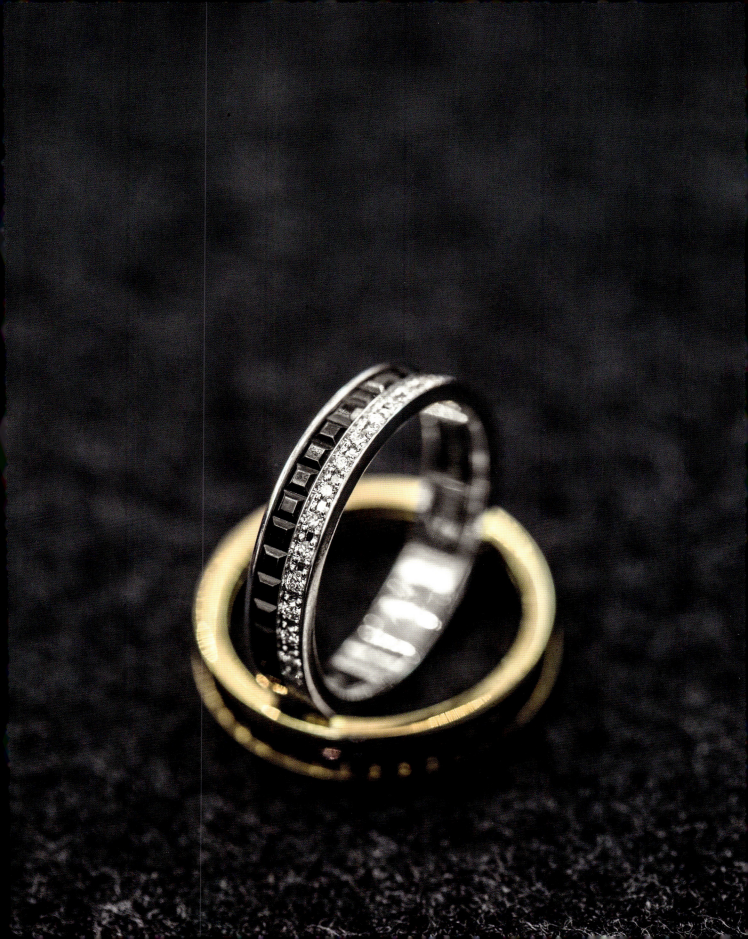

CARTIER

'Cartier absorbed and incorporated the Orient. The influences came, went and replaced one another. Enter the Maharajas. They had money, stones, taste, Western aspirations, fashionable jewels and accessories.'
Cartier and India (2007)

Cartier's pedigree in jewelry for gentlemen is demonstrable in its client list, inscribed in historic ledgers held in London, Paris and New York: Edward VII, Rudolph Valentino, Nicholas II of Russia, Baron de Meyer, Prince Felix Yusupov, the Duke of Windsor, Prince George Duke of Kent, Sir Philip Sassoon, Noël Coward, Cecil Beaton, Richard Burton and Calvin Klein, to name a very few. Although Cartier was established in 1847 and directed by Louis-François Cartier and then his son Alfred, the fashionable jeweler was primarily a retailer of masterpieces made by Foissin, Gueyton, Falize and Boucheron until it moved to 13 Rue de la Paix in 1899, when it began to concentrate on producing its own designs.

Cartier was the first of Paris's high jewelers to have a truly international business. Alfred Cartier's three sons Louis, Pierre and Jacques established independent Cartier town houses in Paris, New York (1909) and London (1902) respectively, eventually establishing their own workshops. In 1904–5 Pierre travelled to St Petersburg and Moscow to sell to the imperial family. In 1911 Jacques travelled to India to complete orders placed for George V's Coronation Durbar in Delhi, and subsequently opened an office there.

The house's designs in the first decade of the twentieth century already show flashes of the avant-garde that would

become a signature. A starkly geometric circular brooch of four calibré-cut rubies framing a tiny central diamond (1909) is unmistakably Cartier. Inspired by the Franco-Egyptian exhibition at the Louvre in 1911, Cartier was the first Parisian jeweler to design pieces in the Egyptian Revival style, and the only house to set ancient scarabs and inscribed faience into jewels and boxes. Cartier also made jewels in the Persian and Indian style from 1913. A masterpiece of the style was a turban tiara set with fifteen emeralds – the largest 177.4cts – in 1926.

Cartier's cliquet pins in the Indian style made in the 1920s lend themselves to a black or midnight-blue grosgrain man's lapel. A double-ended oriental palm-leaf cliquet in carved jade embellished with onyx, white diamonds and rubies in an open-back platinum setting (1923) is a star of Cartier's 1,500-piece 'Cartier Collection' of historic jewels. The Tutti Frutti setting of carved emeralds, sapphires and rubies is the house's most instantly recognizable art deco design and most collectible suite of jewels, including tiaras, bracelets and collars. There is no record of a cufflink set in the Tutti Frutti fashion in the Cartier archives, but dress clips are an option for gentlemen with deep pockets to wear as lapel pins.

The house was fearless in its gem-setting. One of its most successful

Above. Cartier platinum and 18ct white-gold Panther cliquet pin (1957) set with brilliant- and single-cut diamonds, cabochon sapphires and green-garnet eyes.

Opposite. The glamorous Europhile Yashwant Rao Holkar II, Maharaja of Indore, painted in 1934 by Bernard Boutet de Monvel. The jazz-age maharaja was photographed by Man Ray, commissioned the architect Le Corbusier and invited Cartier, Mauboussin and Chaumet to re-set the dynasty's historic jewels.

Preceding pages, left. Cartier's masterpiece double-clip brooch in the Tutti Frutti style made in 1935 for Mrs Cole Porter. Brilliant-, round-, baguette- and single-cut diamonds and carved sapphire, ruby and emerald leaves are set in platinum with calibré-cut rubies, square-carved emeralds and emerald, ruby and sapphire cabochons.

Preceding pages, right. Cartier's Rajasthan brooch in the Tutti Frutti style with a 16.4ct carved Burma sapphire framed by carved rubies, sapphires and emeralds set in platinum with brilliant-cut diamond accents.

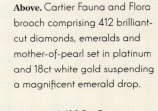

combinations was the Panthère setting of onyx and white diamonds, which first appeared on the bracelet of a watch in 1911. The Panthère has stalked the Cartier high-jewelry collections ever since, and appears in Cartier's contemporary men's collection as a Lying Panther cufflink carved from black onyx with a white-diamond collar, reclining on a bed of 18ct yellow gold. A white-gold Panthère de Cartier link is pavé set with diamonds, with emerald eyes and an onyx nose. A Panthère de Cartier men's dress ring is described in 18ct yellow gold, lacquer, onyx and peridot eyes.

The earliest pieces for men in the Cartier archives (begun in 1970) include a set of bow-motif rose-cut diamond dress studs made in 1902. A yellow-gold cravat slide dated 1902 is extremely rare set with calibré-cut rubies, and an 18ct yellow-and-red-gold 'tank track' bracelet (1945) remains a popular piece for men. Another innovation from the same year in the collection is a pair of cufflinks, one set with a watch, the other a compass.

When we consider Cartier's work throughout the twentieth and twenty-first centuries, it is striking that the language is consistently Cartier while the design studio never repeats itself. For example, it was not until the 1950s that Cartier began creating articulated Panthère jewelry in three dimensions, such as the Duchess of Windsor's diamond, onyx and emerald Panthère bracelet sold by Sotheby's

Above. Cartier Fauna and Flora brooch comprising 412 brilliant-cut diamonds, emeralds and mother-of-pearl set in platinum and 18ct white gold suspending a magnificent emerald drop.

Opposite. A 1930s Cartier Giardinetto brooch set with citrines, emeralds, sapphires and diamonds.

Below. The Cartier 9ct yellow-gold envelope cigarette case (1932) ordered by Sir Winston Churchill for his son Randolph. The stamp is described in red, white and black enamel and the postmark in black enamel. Randolph gave the case to King Farouk of Egypt.

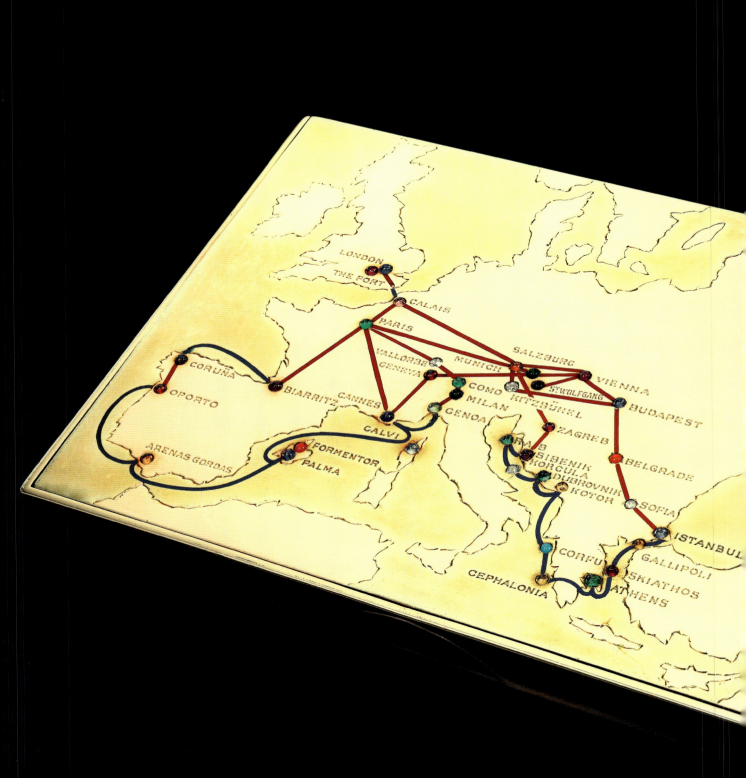

David
from
Wallis

Christmas 1935

'Aldo Cipullo's yellow-gold Nail bangle (1970) for Cartier remains a titan of the contemporary collection, and is also sold as part of the men's collection as cufflinks and rings.'

in 2010 for £4,521,250 from a high estimate of £1,500,000. In 1957 Cartier set a magnificent piece of Panthère jewelry: a prancing big-cat cliquet pin made in brilliant and single-cut diamonds with cabochon-sapphire markings and eyes of green garnet (see page 122). Aldo Cipullo's yellow-gold Nail bangle (1970) for Cartier remains a titan of the contemporary collection, and is also sold as part of the men's collection as cufflinks and rings.

Cartier brings its own provenance to the auction houses, regardless of famous owners. In 2017 Sotheby's sold a sapphire-set moonstone dress set comprising cufflinks, four buttons and four studs, dated about

1920, for $13,750, from a high estimate of $7,000. In the same year it sold an openwork circular design rose-cut-diamond and platinum cufflink for $7,500. Men seeking Cartier treasures may be wise to look at pieces of antique jewelry that may not be considered fashionable for women, but that make devastatingly chic lapel pins, such as the sapphire-and-diamond arrow jabot pin Bonhams sold for £6,000 in 2017, or a marvellous yellow-gold dahlia brooch (1958) it sold in the same year for £9,375.

www.cartier.co.uk

Preceding pages. The Duke of Windsor's Cartier gold gem-set cigarette case sold at Sotheby's in 2010 for £181,250. The inscription reads 'David from Wallis Christmas 1935'.

Opposite. The actor Jared Leto pinned a sapphire-and-diamond brooch (1957) by Cartier to his Gucci shirt collar for the 2016 Met Gala in New York.

Below. Cartier platinum and brilliant-cut diamond cufflinks set with two magnificent Ceylon sapphires with a total weight of 7.2ct.

VAN CLEEF & ARPELS

'Van Cleef & Arpels was not merely a purveyor of jewels to these men and women who possessed – and still possess – colossal fortunes, but also their confidant.'

Vincent Meylan, *Van Cleef & Arpels: Treasures and Legends* (2011)

Van Cleef & Arpels arrived on the Place Vendôme in Paris in 1906 following the marriage of Alfred van Cleef, a stonecutter's son, and Estelle Arpels, daughter of a precious-stone dealer. The firm was founded by Alfred with Estelle's brother Charles Arpels. Within two decades the house had established itself as one of the most dynamic, creative forces in fine jewelry. It blossomed in the carefree 1920s, when Paris led the world with art deco jewelry drawing on Egyptian and Indian influences.

Despite the Wall Street Crash of 1929, Van Cleef entered a golden era of creativity in the 1930s thanks to its artistic director, Renée Puissant (Alfred and Estelle's daughter), and designer René Sim Lacaze. During this time the minaudière was invented – a gold, bejeweled handheld vanity case containing gold clocks, lighters, lipsticks, pillboxes, compacts and notebooks – and the Mystery Setting patented (1933). Inspired by Roman micro-mosaics, the latter enabled precious stones to be placed edge to edge without the grid-like gold setting beneath being visible. Jewelry could be partially mystery-set, for example in the Ludo bracelets (a nickname for Louis Arpels, Alfred's brother-in-law) with their mystery-set ruby clasps resembling belt buckles.

In 1937 the house made an extraordinary Jaretière bracelet, a vast swirl of faceted rubies surrounded by diamonds, for the actress Marlene Dietrich, who famously wore it in Alfred Hitchcock's *Stage Fright* in 1950. The sheer variety of designs that emerged from Van Cleef in the 1930s is exceptional. The firm embraced modernism with radically chic and minimal jewels, such as the 18ct yellow-gold Chapeau Chinoise collar, bracelet and earrings, and three-dimensional white-diamond bows set with brilliant- and baguette-cut diamonds.

The firm's first foray into New York was scuppered by the Crash, but the house maintained an office there from 1939. In 1944 it opened a boutique at 744 Fifth Avenue. Louis and his wife, the model Hélène Ostrowska, were forced to flee Paris with Charles in 1940, and settled in New York. Tragically, Puissant took her own life in 1942, a month after the German invasion of Vichy.

One of the most intriguing collaborations emerged from the friendship of balletomane Claude Arpels and New York City Ballet founder and choreographer George Balanchine. Van Cleef had been making jeweled ballerina and fairy clips since the early 1940s. They inspired Balanchine's ballet *Jewels* (1967), a three-act performance depicting emeralds, rubies and diamonds with music by Fauré, Stravinsky and Tchaikovsky. Van Cleef's goldwork in the late 1940s was a show of optimism and

Opposite. Horst. P. Horst's jewelry shoot for Vogue in 1935, displaying pieces of haute joaillerie by Van Cleef & Arpels.

Overleaf. A Van Cleef & Arpels 18ct white-gold, grey mother-of-pearl and diamond Butterfly clip. Tailoring by Henry Poole & Co.

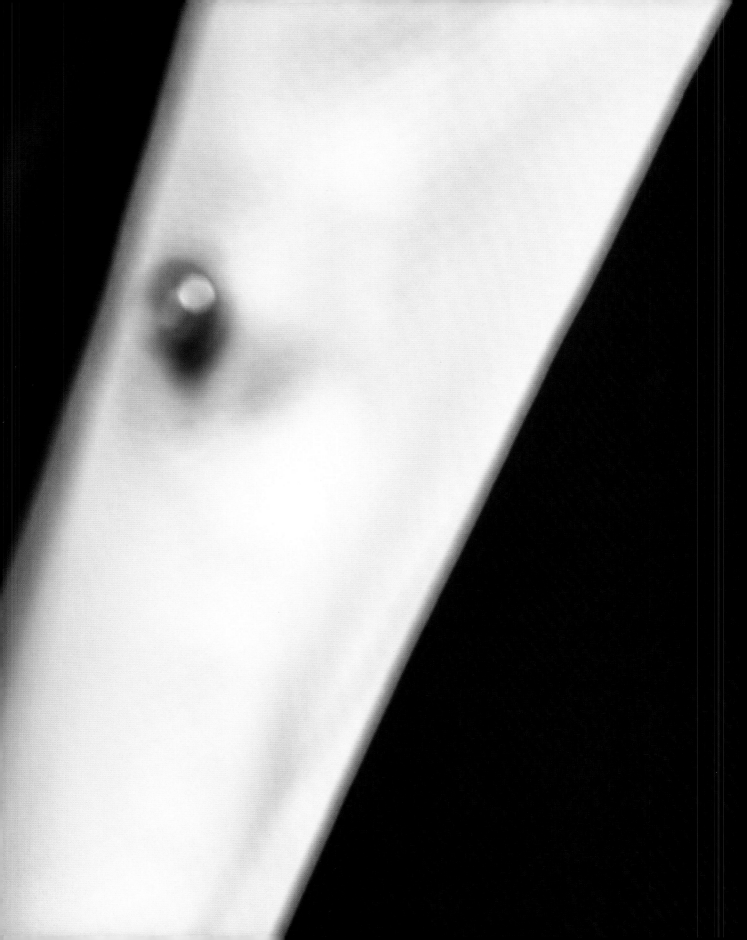

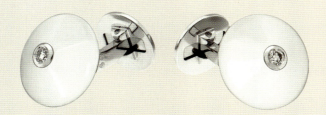

extravagance, as befits the American influence, with coloured stones and yellow gold. The latter was worked into lace-like clips encrusted with white diamonds and polished gold floral brooches with three-dimensional petals set with rubies and diamonds that would look handsome on a gentleman's lapel.

Van Cleef has an unprecedented record among Parisian high jewelers for setting crown jewels after the Second World War, when it was directed by second-generation Arpels brothers Claude, Jacques and Pierre. The cantankerous Sita Devi, Maharani of Baroda, chain-smoked thin cigars at 22 Place Vendôme while Jacques showed her a magnificent Lotus Flower collar of cabochons and carved emeralds and diamonds. Prince Rainier of Monaco commissioned a pearl and diamond parure as a wedding gift for

the actress Grace Kelly in 1956. In 1967 Empress Farah Diba of Iran was crowned with a diamond, pearl and carved-emerald diadem that weighed nearly 2 kilograms (4½ lb). Van Cleef also set jewels for Eva Perón, Barbara Hutton, Maria Callas, Ava Gardner, Jackie Onassis and Elizabeth Taylor.

The house's prolific output of the 1960s and 1970s is a particularly rich seam for male collectors. The Bird of Paradise clip (1963) is an elegant and lovingly described creature rendered in yellow gold, platinum, brilliant-cut diamonds, faceted rubies, sapphires and navette-cut emeralds. In 1954 Van Cleef had opened La Boutique at 22 Place Vendôme, selling a more youthful, accessible collection of jewelry, and shortly afterwards it began designing humorous animal-motif clips that became wildly popular in the 1960s.

Above. Agate-and-diamond Pierre Arpels Pastilles cufflinks by Van Cleef & Arpels, set in 18ct white gold.

Opposite. Van Cleef & Arpels Cosmos 18ct white-gold and diamond flower clip pendant. Tailoring by Henry Poole & Co.

Below. Van Cleef & Arpels 18ct yellow-gold and mother-of-pearl Alhambra cufflinks.

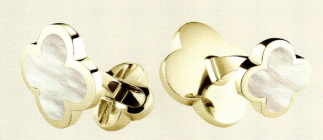

'Van Cleef's commitment in recent years to producing collections of high jewelry has been impressive.'

Van Cleef & Arpels Rose de Noël clips in 18ct yellow gold, white mother-of-pearl and diamonds and 18ct white gold, grey mother-of-pearl and diamonds.

During the 1960s a menagerie of Van Cleef animals appeared: a figured yellow-gold-and-diamond Lapin with cabochon-onyx eye and coral carrot in its mouth; a coral, emerald and diamond Squirrel with a bushy yellow-gold tail; and a gold, enamel and diamond Giraffe. In 1968 Van Cleef introduced the Alhambra long necklace in a four-leaf clover design that has since been set in every conceivable hardstone and works particularly well as a cufflink (see p.136).

From 2000, Van Cleef was no longer in Arpels family hands, since the Swiss-based luxury-goods group Richemont had bought a majority stake. The commitment in recent years to producing collections of high jewelry has been impressive. Interestingly, the Arche de Noé (Noah's Ark) high jewelry (2016) is led by pairs of clips that can be worn and collected by male or female devotees of the Van Cleef style. Animals are depicted two-by-two in amusing, elegant designs in hardstones, diamonds and enamel, and could conceivably land on a gentleman's cocktail suit.

The salerooms are relatively favourable for men's jewelry by Van Cleef. In 2016 Sotheby's sold a seven-baton set of yellow-gold and diamond links (including onyx, tiger's eye, malachite, lapis lazuli, rock crystal and carnelian) for £8,500, from a high estimate of £7,000. Prices skyrocket for famous designs, such as the mystery-set ruby-and-diamond Three Leaves brooch Bonhams New York sold in 2016 for $342,000. In 2017 Sotheby's Hong Kong sold a ruby, diamond, sapphire and emerald Bird of Paradise brooch set in yellow gold for 287,500HKD.

www.vancleefarpels.com

CHAPTER FOUR

LAPEL PINS AND BROOCHES

—

LAPEL PINS AND BROOCHES

'No matter whether a piece of jewelry was originally chosen for its amuletic purpose, its attractiveness or its social cache, it probably always has one special quality: it could be used as a form of currency, almost as an investment.'

Hugh Tait (ed.), *7,000 Years of Jewellery* (2006)

The lapel pin, a brooch in all but name, is the largest and most flamboyant piece of jewelry in a chap's artillery. Although not exclusively reserved for after the cocktail hour, a gem-set lapel pin is one's opportunity to bow to the Indian maharajas' influence on jewelry for gentlemen. When wearing black tie, white tie or a smoking jacket, anything goes, from white-diamond knife-wire-set belle époque crescents, starbursts and butterflies to Andrew Grima's yellow-gold cast Pencil Shaving brooch (see page 233) scattered with brilliant-cut diamonds (1968) via the art deco beauty of a carved emerald and diamond bay-tree belonging to Bentley & Skinner.

The red carpet at the Academy Awards in 2017 marked a turning point in providing credible role models for men's jewelry. *Once Upon a Time* Prince Charming Josh Dallas wore a yellow-and-white-gold rose pin in his lapel and gold dress studs that had a casual elegance reminiscent of Fred Astaire. Pharrell Williams twinned multiple ropes of black Chanel pearls with a white-diamond Catherine-wheel brooch that was a major leap into high jewelry for a hip-hop idol. *Hidden Figures* actor Aldis Hodge pinned a silver and jet festoon chain from breast pocket to lapel, and wore a suite of matching silver rings and bracelets. This multicultural triumvirate brought men's jewelry to a mainstream global audience.

Unsurprisingly, the fashion peacocks were early adopters of the lapel pin. At the Met Gala in 2013, US *Vogue*'s international editor-at-large, Hamish Bowles, pinned the lapels of his Tom Ford tuxedo with a suite of 100 jewels designed exclusively for the event by star stylist David Thomas and made by Jason of Beverly Hills. The white-gold and emerald shirt studs and cufflinks were relatively conventional, however exquisite, but the lapel pins were extraordinary: sixty-four white-gold, diamond and emerald safety pins of varying sizes, two white-gold and emerald kilt pins and two diamond fleur-de-lys stick pins.

The American fashion designer Zac Posen has worn significant antique gem-set brooches to the Met Gala for many years. He favours nineteenth-century white-diamond jewels in the scroll and garland styles, as well as coral brooches from the 1940s. For the ball in 2016, 'Manus x Machina: Fashion in the Age of Technology', the singer Nick Jonas

Page 140. The fashion designer Zac Posen accompanies the model Tao Okamoto to the opening of the Metropolitan Opera Season in New York in 2014. He is wearing an art deco diamond clip as a lapel pin.

Above. This Tiffany & Co. 18ct rose-gold safety-pin brooch set with brilliant-cut diamonds was sold by Bonhams London in 2016 for £5,250.

Opposite. Hamish Bowles and Sarah Jessica Parker on the red carpet for the 2006 Met Gala, 'Punk: Chaos to Couture', in New York. Bowles is wearing a suite of bespoke safety-pin jewelry designed by David Thomas.

Overleaf. Edwardian diamond scroll brooch from Bentley & Skinner, comprising three old brilliant-cut diamonds in a flowing openwork diamond-set surround (c.1901). Tailoring by Turnbull & Asser.

Above. A contemporary platinum-mounted diamond-set brooch by Wartski, consisting of three interlocking triangles. Tailoring by Henry Poole & Co.

Opposite. A Victorian diamond twelve-ray star brooch from Bentley & Skinner, centred on a 0.65ct old brilliant-cut diamond (c.1870). Tailoring by Henry Poole & Co.

commissioned the London-based avant-garde jeweler Husam El Odeh to create a lapel pin featuring microchips and semi-precious stones set in silver. Bowles and Jonas are working in the great tradition of the golden-age Hollywood stars who commissioned jewels from Flato, Verdura, Cartier and Van Cleef & Arpels.

In 2006 Alexander McQueen wore matching black Tahitian pearl and black spinel Thistle brooches made by Shaun Leane to the Met Ball's 'AngloMania' gala (see page 76). Although large, the glittering, dark sheen of the black rhodium-plated silver setting makes Thistle into a pleasing masculine brooch.

As with all things masculine, size clearly does matter for lapel pins and brooches. There is a limit to what even a generous jacket lapel can take, although it is gratifying to push that limit when the brooch is a novelty such as Hancocks' supersized nineteenth-century gold, silver, diamond and cabochon-tiger's-eye bee (see page 204). Bentley & Skinner's oval cabochon-garnet and rose-cut diamond beetle with ruby eyes (1890) is a more modest jewel, but a miniature masterpiece nonetheless (see page 196). Theo Fennell's white-gold, sapphire, diamond and black-diamond bee brooch is made to scale and pins neatly on to the buttonhole (see page 55).

Celestial, botanical, animal and insect motif brooches created for ladies in the nineteenth and twentieth centuries translate beautifully to a cocktail suit or DJ lapel. Bentley & Skinner's inventory has a generous helping of terribly pretty white-diamond jewelry, such as a Victorian diamond star brooch with a central stone of 0.65ct surrounded by twelve rays set with graduating old-cut diamonds; it echoes a royal decoration when worn on the breast pocket of a velvet dinner jacket. A white-diamond butterfly from 1890 with a magnificent wingspan is set with 16ct of old brilliant- and rose-cut stones, with a flash of ruby in the eyes.

The prettiness and delicacy of a modest belle époque white-diamond butterfly, dragonfly, lizard or bird design add just the right touch of sparkle to a grosgrain or satin lapel, whereas the more geometric art deco style benefits from being an eye-popping combination of gemstones. Yet more minimal, contemporary designs can be taken to the max, such

as Stephen Webster's large white-diamond pavé-set openwork butterfly brooch, Fly by Night (see page 92), or Van Cleef & Arpels' streamlined grey mother-of-pearl butterfly (see page 134). That said, time and fashion have made small but perfectly formed jewels, such as Bentley & Skinner's Fonsèque et Olive frosted green-glass and diamond grape brooch of 1889, a much easier sell to men than to women.

Naturalistic designs lend themselves to a gentleman's brooch. The 'Delicious Jewels' collection by the fourth-generation Munich fine jeweler Hemmerle included a miraculous Peas in a Pod pin, described in green tsavorite, garnets and white gold, with peas made from balls of green jade. It is the perfect *amuse-bouche* for the lapel, as are Hemmerle's Cauliflower and Sweet Corn brooches (see page 237). Michele della Valle's jeweled exotic fish could be worn in the spirit of Hamish Bowles as a shoal, while the yellow-diamond and green-garnet leaping frog by the Japanese jeweler Gimel is a bravura colour drift of gemstones. In 1982 the great JAR set arguably the most innovative naturalistic brooch: in Poppy, the stem of a red-and-green tourmaline flower twines around a substantial pear-shaped diamond.

With the exception of Solange Azagury-Partridge, who imbues all her creations with humour, it seems that there is little amusement to be found in jewels today. If we work on the premise that men might wear an after-dark piece of fine jewelry to amuse or seduce, we must look back to the eras when the fine jeweler created talking-point pieces, such as the fascinating yellow-gold owl brooch belonging to Wartski, designed by Paul Robin in 1890 with a wise cabochon-tiger's-eye stare and rose-cut diamonds peppering the circular pin. Hancocks has a menagerie of amusing animals and birds, including a mid-twentieth-century textured gold owl lapel pin with platinum claws and cabochon-ruby eyes, and a Van Cleef & Arpels yellow-gold elephant with emerald-set eyes.

The jewelers of the nineteenth and twentieth centuries understood that a jewel had the power to speak and that the level of sophistication was there to make ordering jewelry an act of courtship. Lucas Rarities has a bow-and-arrow design attributed to Paul Flato, described in 14ct yellow gold, diamonds and rubies and designed to be worn shooting the golden

Above. A Paul Robin tiger's-eye, diamond and gold owl brooch (c.1880–90) from Wartski.

Opposite. An Edwardian naturalistic dragonfly brooch from Bentley & Skinner. The delicate wings are set with diamonds, the tail with emeralds and the head with a natural pearl, with cabochon-ruby eyes mounted in yellow gold.

Overleaf. A magnificently sculpted owl brooch (c.1950) from Hancocks, finely modelled in 18ct yellow gold with platinum talons and cabochon-ruby eyes.

'Realistically, no chap is going to wear a large sparkling showpiece pin or brooch before dark, any more than a lady would wear a tiara. But exquisite goldwork, enamel and opaque hardstones are eminently applicable to daytime jewelry for gentlemen.'

arrow straight to the wearer's heart (see page 43). A favourite piece in Wartski's collection is an old brilliant-cut diamond and ruby quiver-of-arrows brooch dated *c*.1890, made to hold two removable jeweled arrows (see page 112). The arrows were to be pinned to a lover's lapel in the hope that he or she wouldn't leave the ball without the promise of another assignation.

While discussing the market for fine jewelry with the antiques dealer Harry Fane, it was interesting to learn that the fashion for bar brooches – such as his oriental art deco sapphire-and-diamond pin by Boucheron (see page 120) – garners more interest from men than women. It is easy to see why when it is pinned to the top pocket of a suit, where it sits perfectly. Wartski's Tiffany target brooch of 1930, comprising four intersecting circles of white gold set with brilliant-cut blue sapphires and diamonds, absolutely sang out when pinned to the pocket of Turnbull & Asser's blue-and-black silk jacquard dinner jacket. Fulco di Verdura's Byzantine yellow-gold and coloured-stone cross brooch made for Chanel in about 1930, inspired by the Ravenna mosaics, is both magnificent and masculine when worn like a royal order from a Ruritanian Balkan state (see page 175).

The richest source of gentlemen's brooches from ladies' designs is the garden of floral motifs that every jewel house has visited in its own unique fashion. The Giardinetto (see page 127) is perhaps the most appropriate lapel pin, because of the late nineteenth-century precedent for men to wear a flower in the lapel. Cartier excelled at the flower-vase brooch, such as the 1930s piece in the Hancocks inventory set with diamonds, sapphires, citrines and carved emeralds (see page 127). A flower-vase brooch is the jeweler's excuse to mix a bouquet of coloured gemstones. One of the prettiest is Wartski's unsigned diamond flower vase from 1935, with ruby, sapphire, citrine and amethyst blooms, all centred with a white diamond (see page 209).

Flower motifs challenge the jeweler to work in three dimensions. Each yellow-gold petal of a Van Cleef & Arpels flower clip (above) is expertly curled, and interspersed with brilliant-cut diamonds and faceted rubies or sapphires. In a contemporary pink-gold Cartier Magicien lapel pin, the flower is sculpted from pink chalcedony and the stem decorated with pink

Above. A Van Cleef & Arpels polished 18ct yellow-gold, diamond and sapphire flower brooch (*c*.1955).

Opposite. The Black Rose: a brooch by Leon Coulon (*c*.1900) described in layered pierced-silver petals mounted with rose-cut diamonds. Courtesy of Wartski.

Left. A bird in flight brooch by Pierre Sterlé (c.1970). The body is set with a cabochon aquamarine and the wings and tail are fashioned from gold thread scattered with round brilliant-cut diamonds. The head is set with round sapphires and diamonds.

Overleaf. A late Victorian gold double-cherub brooch signed by Boucheron, spearing a heart-cut diamond accented with ruby flames. Courtesy of Wartski.

Opposite. An elegant gold leaf brooch scattered with round brilliant-cut diamonds by Pierre Sterlé (c.1950). Courtesy of Hancocks. Tailoring by Henry Poole & Co.

Below. A diamond tree jabot pin from Bentley & Skinner, set with baguette- and old-cut diamonds in platinum (c.1920).

sapphires and diamonds. The contours of Van Cleef & Arpels' Rose de Noël clips, in white or grey mother-of-pearl accented with diamonds and yellow gold, are plump, tactile and pleasing to the eye (see page 138).

Realistically, no chap is going to wear a large sparkling showpiece pin or brooch before dark, any more than a lady would wear a tiara. But exquisite goldwork, enamel and opaque hardstones are eminently applicable to daytime jewelry for gentlemen. Few will criticize a figurative Lalique art nouveau pin, such as the gold-and-enamel Nymph pin in the Hancocks collection. Grima past or present is also a safe bet worn with tweeds: Andrew Grima's stalactite and stalagmite 18ct yellow-gold and diamond brooch, perhaps, or Jojo Grima's abstract twig of figured yellow gold and diamonds (see page 234).

The more yellow gold dominates a design or the more intricate the jewel work, the further a brooch ventures into safe waters for daytime wear. The Panthère de Cartier is a prime example. Less familiar but even more collectible are Cartier's tigers, introduced by its creative director Jeanne Toussaint in the 1950s, inspired by her tiger-skin coat. Popular with the American heiress Barbara Hutton and the Duchess of Windsor, Cartier's tigers are expressive creatures. In 2015 Bonhams sold a handsome prowling tiger from 1990, with emerald eyes and a body striped with onyx and orange, yellow and near colourless diamond pavé shading, for £64,900.

Brooches and lapel pins for men are still a burgeoning market for the antiques dealers and auction houses, and the strongest designs tend to resonate more with men, such as a haematite oriental lady's head and shoulders wearing an exaggerated peridot- and citrine-set turban topped with diamond plumes, formerly in the Hancocks inventory. The bold handwriting of the mid-century Parisian marque Pierre Sterlé is pleasing to male collectors, who appreciate the ingenuity of his yellow-gold and gemstone bird brooches or his 1950s roped yellow-gold leaf brooches scattered with round brilliant-cut diamonds, also owned by Hancocks. The only limit in the choice of a jeweled man's brooch or lapel pin is the imagination, and of course the wallet.

DAVID YURMAN

'I think every man should embrace wearing jewelry in his daily life.'

Evan Yurman

Founded in 1980 by husband and wife David and Sybil Yurman, David Yurman has emerged as a world leader in men's jewelry, largely thanks to the couple's creative powerhouse of a son, the house's chief design director, Evan Yurman. Since joining the family business in 2003, Evan has shown a total commitment to broadening the horizon of contemporary men's jewelry: pioneering new materials such as fused meteorite, forged carbon, titanium and dinosaur bone; reimagining ancient crafts such as carving hardstones; and raising the game by producing high jewelry for men, such as the suite of Shipwreck textured yellow-gold rings, cufflinks and dress studs (2017) embedded with multicoloured precious stones.

'I get bored if I don't work with interesting materials: meteorite, black titanium, grey titanium, cold moulded rubber, you name it,' says Evan. 'The amount of custom work we do for men is off the scale. I have made dinosaur claws with alexandrite, 30ct opal rings, Burma ruby rings, a bracelet that contained a pound of platinum.' When he took control of the men's collections, he started to explore the higher reaches of fine jewelry.

Such is Evan's belief in fine men's jewelry that in January 2017 he showcased the collection in Milan's deconsecrated Baroque church of San Paolo Converso, for Men's Fashion Week. Unique pieces on display included a ring set with a second-century intaglio of Emperor Commodus in a setting inspired by gladiatorial armour, and a substantial diamond with a star inclusion set in a platinum dress ring.

When we meet at the monolithic David Yurman HQ in New York's Tribeca district, the men's collection is on show in a dimly lit concrete men's den with an array of motorbikes gleaming in the dark and a table loaded with minerals, ammonites, meteorites and crystals: a blueprint if ever there was one for a standalone David Yurman Man flagship. 'It's got to be in New York,' says Evan. 'My dad was born here, I grew up here. Actually, I grew up in my mum and dad's studio. I've been designing from the age of fourteen. I had school to deal with, which was really annoying. My father gave me the option of college or work, and I chose work. When I arrived, there was a very small offering for men. I thought men needed more options.'

Evan is a prolific designer, also responsible for designing timepieces, wedding jewels and the high-jewelry women's collection he introduced in 2010. 'I started the more expensive division, making jewelry in gold, diamonds and gemstones,' he says, 'and we basically upgraded our clients. They loved the gold and we gave them something else to buy. When you design jewelry, you do want to make pieces in precious metal and gemstones that in fifty to a hundred years from now will have significance. But we've also got to be commercial.'

Above. The David Yurman 18ct sterling silver Meteorite signet ring.

Opposite. The actor Chris Pine attends the Cannes Film Festival in 2016 wearing a sterling silver David Yurman signet ring.

Above. The David Yurman Petrvs Bee signet ring in 18ct yellow gold.

Opposite. The David Yurman Petrvs Scarab signet ring with carved carnelian set in 22ct yellow gold. Tailoring by Turnbull & Asser.

Overleaf, clockwise from left. David Yurman 18ct yellow-gold Shipwreck coin amulet mounted on an 18ct yellow-gold fluted chain; David Yurman 18ct yellow-gold and cabochon-ruby dress-stud set designed by Evan Yurman for the Shipwreck collection; David Yurman Shipwreck dress rings in textured 18ct yellow gold set with cabochon emeralds, sapphires and rubies, designed by Evan Yurman.

Despite being an obsessive petrol head, Evan Yurman makes men's jewelry that does not fall into the cliché of biker, rocker or heavy metal. It is undeniably masculine, but David Yurman jewelry has an elegance that can come only from a man with a meticulously archived collection of intriguing antique jewelry (Victorian stick pins, Roman rings, masonic pins, ancient coins, carved jade) catalogued in his studio. Elegance with edge is perhaps the reason why David Yurman is the go-to men's jeweler for red-carpet appearances. Chris Pine, Brad Pitt, Justin Timberlake, Liam Hemsworth, Will Smith, Joel Edgerton, Jeremy Piven, Justin Bieber, Zayn Malik and Leonardo DiCaprio – the last of whom wore Yurman platinum braided-knot short studs to the Academy Awards in 2014 – all choose David Yurman as their gentlemen's jeweler.

Although David Yurman is now a multimillion-dollar global business, it remains a family affair with a cool, beatnik backstory. David Yurman was living in Greenwich Village and working as an apprentice to the sculptor Jacques Lipchitz when he met Sybil, who was also a sculptor. Their lives became 'intertwined by love and art', and David created for Sybil a bronze Dante necklace that led to a small artisan jewelry business, selling at arts-and-crafts fairs across America. They married in 1979 and had intended to sell the business on the afternoon of the ceremony. With an offer too low and doubts voiced by the buyer, they walked away – Sybil still wearing bridal flowers in her hair – and in 1980 they formed David Yurman. One of their first designs, the yellow-gold and diamond Starlight necklace, won the World Gold Council's Jury Award in the same year, and formed the blueprint for the house's icon Cable design.

The Cable has featured in every collection since. In 2010, in celebration of the firm's thirtieth anniversary, David Yurman opened its breathtaking five-storey town house on Madison Avenue, with its famous cable-inspired staircase and door handles sculpted by David Yurman. In 2013 Evan celebrated his first decade as the key creative leader in the design of the men's collection. 'Every collection, I am asking guys to come with me on the journey,' he says.

There is a Gotham sensibility to David Yurman men's jewelry that could be fed only by the downtown Manhattan vibe. Evan can take a large, faceted hessonite garnet that would bling in yellow gold but which sits like a superhero's ring when set in sterling silver and steel. One sees the same tension between up- and downtown in four sterling-silver dress studs made in chunks of meteorite, or the nut-and-bolt shape of Streamline cufflinks in 18ct yellow gold and silver. That said, as a body of work David Yurman men's jewelry defies classification by age or profession.

'I seem to have hit the right note. Nobody else is doing what we are doing, and the jewelry isn't derivative. We have a lot of fun with materials. In fact, we have a lot of fun.'

Evan Yurman

'It was my dad's model to make jewelry for all kinds of people,' says Evan, 'and that works both ways, hence the introduction of the high-jewelry collection. The demand for precious men's jewelry was coming from our clients. I know that if we make a diamond dress set, there's going to be the client who will enjoy it. You'll see Wall Street guys at the Metropolitan Opera wearing our gold Cable cufflinks. He might be the same guy wearing one of our pendants or bracelets at a music festival. You can't stereotype men as having one style any more. That's not the way we live.'

'Jewelry is talismanic,' Evan continues, 'particularly if it has been bought or made by your friends and family.' On why David Yurman men's jewelry has gone into orbit, he says, 'I seem to have hit the right note. Nobody else is doing what we are doing, and the jewelry isn't derivative. We have a lot of fun with materials. In fact, we have a lot of fun. We have a strong commercial business – with about 65,000 pieces in the mainline – and that allows us to get creative.'

www.davidyurman.com

Opposite, top. David Yurman Shipwreck sterling silver coin rings.

Opposite, bottom. A David Yurman Shipwreck sterling silver chain bracelet and necklace.

Below. The David Yurman 18ct yellow-gold Forged Carbon cufflinks.

TIFFANY & Co.

> 'The beguiling sound of the word Tiffany conjures up images of a light-hearted and immensely pleasurable world. It stands for glamour, fine craftsmanship and lively design. To us on this side of the Atlantic it is also quintessentially American in character.'
>
> Lord Rothschild, foreword to *Bejewelled by Tiffany 1837–1987* (2006)

Founded on Broadway in 1837, the firm that was christened Tiffany & Co. in 1853 is unique in the high-jewelry firmament for appointing a succession of brave, brilliant designers whose names appeared with equal billing: the founder's son Louis Comfort Tiffany (1902), Jean Schlumberger (1956), Donald Claflin (1965), Elsa Peretti (1974), Paloma Picasso (1980) and Frank Gehry (2000). These guest stars, working latterly with Tiffany & Co.'s design director emeritus John Loring, brought wit, verve, energy and uniqueness to the house's many styles of jewelry for gentlemen.

Although only ten years separate the birth of the New World fine jeweler Tiffany & Co. (1837) and its transatlantic rival Cartier (1847), the former's founder, Charles Lewis Tiffany, was a man of many firsts. New York's 'King of Diamonds' opened a Paris office in 1850, almost sixty years before Cartier arrived in Manhattan, and was in London from 1872, thirty years before Cartier opened its boutique there. Tiffany bought more than a third of the French crown jewels when they were auctioned in 1887, and they were devoured by socially ambitious American heiresses. In the second half of the nineteenth century Tiffany & Co. counted the kings of Prussia, Belgium, Italy, Denmark, Greece, Spain, Portugal and Romania as clients, as well as Queen Victoria and the emperors of Russia and Austria.

But, like Cartier, Tiffany & Co. as we recognize it today took flight only with the turn of the twentieth century. On the death of his father in 1902, Louis Comfort Tiffany was made art director of the family firm. His naturalistic, delicate art nouveau designs largely eschewed faceted gemstones in favour of gold filigree settings, enamel embellishment, misty stones such as opal or mother-of-pearl and hardstones such as turquoise and jade. The technique and colour drifts were identical to the stained glass Tiffany & Co. was producing during the same period. Drawing directly from nature, Tiffany would copy the fretwork of a dragonfly's wings or Queen Anne's lace flower head in yellow gold for brooches and hair ornaments.

Louis Comfort Tiffany resigned as artistic director in 1918, making his jewelry as rare as hen's teeth today and thus reaching stratospheric sums. In 2017 Sotheby's New York sold a black-opal, enamel and coloured-stone parure for $125,000 and an opal, sapphire and 18ct yellow-gold brooch for $75,000. An 18ct yellow-gold, lapis lazuli, emerald and coloured-diamond Louis Comfort Tiffany brooch made for a man's lapel was sold at the same auction for $11,250, from a high estimate of $8,000.

Jean Schlumberger was discovered by the great Parisian surrealist couturier

Above. An exquisite Tiffany & Co. miniature umbrella stick pin (c.1935) with graduated calibré-cut emeralds set in platinum. An articulated brilliant-cut diamond raindrop is suspended at the end of each rib.

Opposite. This Donald Claflin for Tiffany & Co. Lily of the Valley brooch (c.1969) was sold at Bonhams New York in 2017 for $10,000. Eleven *en tremblant* lilies are set with round brilliant-cut diamonds on a gold stem with green-enamel leaves.

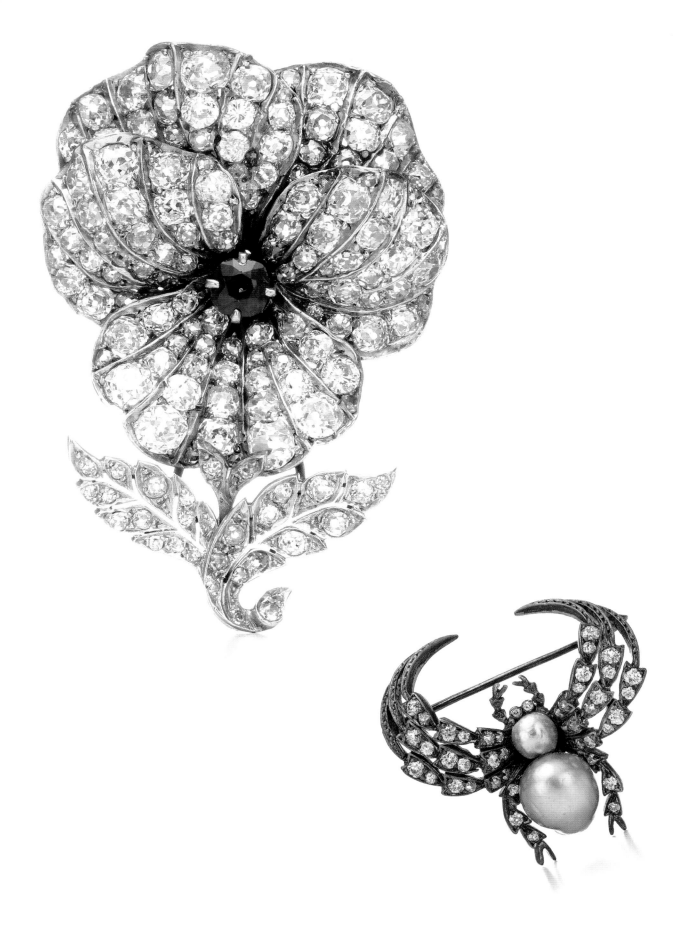

Elsa Schiaparelli and joined Tiffany & Co. in 1956, a year after the company was taken over by the Hoving Corporation and its charismatic leader, Walter Hoving. Schlumberger's masterpiece was the Bird on a Rock setting for the 128.54ct Tiffany fancy yellow diamond. The brooch setting has an 18ct yellow-gold, white- and yellow-diamond fanciful bird with a ruby eye perched inquisitively on top of the claw-set stone. A much-reduced version of the Bird on a Rock, with a citrine, sold at Sotheby's New York in 2016 for $37,500. Although it is open season in the twenty-first century for men to wear Schlumberger's brooches, he did design many pieces for men that are still in production today and embody his creed to 'capture the irregularity of the universe'.

The spirit of Schiaparelli is evident in one of Schlumberger's most popular cufflink designs. The Acorn is a double-headed bar link with pearly grey haematite acorns sitting in cups of 18ct yellow gold (see page 15). Tiffany & Co. also continue

to produce Schlumberger's 18ct yellow-gold bar-and-ball Woven Knot cufflinks, with textured gold that mimicks a knot in a rope. Antique Schlumberger cufflinks from the 1960s and 1970s are much sought after and touch the £10,000 mark, such as his yellow-gold flying-fish bar-and-ball links with emerald eyes and scales described in 18ct yellow gold, or his 18ct yellow-gold twisted Cornucopia horns set with cabochon lapis lazuli.

Donald Claflin's work for Tiffany & Co. tends to be overlooked, coinciding as it does with that of Schlumberger, but his whimsical novelty brooches made for the house between 1965 and 1977 are masterpieces in miniature. Claflin worked in the realm of fairy tale and children's stories, constructing incredibly complex jewels inspired by such characters as Humpty Dumpty, Stuart Little and the Walrus in *Alice in Wonderland*. The humour is a smokescreen for the bravura display of lapidary techniques, as in a frog brooch from 1966 in which the gold-

Preceding pages. A Tiffany & Co. white-gold brooch in the form of four intersecting circles, each centred with a brilliant-cut diamond and set with concentric circles of brilliant-cut blue sapphires and diamonds (c.1930).

Left. Elsa Peretti for Tiffany & Co. 18ct yellow-gold Circle cufflinks.

and turquoise-set amphibian claps its diamond hands around a large turquoise, its emerald eyes popping.

Claflin's pieces for Tiffany & Co. light up salerooms. His 18ct yellow-gold, platinum, coloured-stone and diamond Basilisk brooch (c.1970) sold at Sotheby's New York for $46,875 from a high estimate of $12,000, while his threaded yellow-gold, diamond and emerald Face of Bacchus brooch sold at Bonhams New York in 2012 for $36,250.

When the Italian Elsa Peretti joined Tiffany & Co. in 1974, she drew a definitive line under whimsy and baroque in favour of a radical 'sport couture' chic line of jewelry that has travelled terribly well into the twenty-first century. Peretti pursued simplicity just as Schlumberger and Claflin indulged in fireworks of complexity rendered in precious stones and metal. Her rallying call was 'Nothing is new. Good lines and good forms are timeless.' Her first design for Tiffany & Co., Diamonds by the Yard, threw away the preciousness of faceted diamonds in a fine gold chain set at irregular intervals with single brilliant-cut diamonds. Worn at Studio 54 by the Manhattan divas Liza Minnelli and Bianca Jagger, Diamonds by the Yard is a simple design that twenty-first-century men can and do wear with supreme confidence.

Peretti's sterling silver bean shape has since been interpreted as the drop of a pendant or the terminal of a cufflink in white, rose and yellow gold. The Peretti style is intentionally bisexual, as was the wont of Manhattan society in the 1970s, and still speaks to Tiffany's male clients today.

www.tiffany.co.uk

Below. Donald Claflin for Tiffany & Co. gold, diamond, pink tourmaline, citrine, coral and turquoise Aztec brooch (1967).

Left. This diamond and 18ct yellow-gold Pinecone brooch by Donald Claflin for Tiffany & Co. was sold by Bonhams New York in 2017 for $10,000.

Right. Donald Claflin for Tiffany & Co. gold, platinum, diamond, ruby, emerald and turquoise Dragon brooch (1967).

VERDURA

'In her gossip columns and how-to-entertain books, [Elsa] Maxwell, the famous international hostess, never failed to heap fulsome praise upon Fulco, whom she selected as one of the eleven international personalities whose presence around her dinner table would guarantee "the most perfect party imaginable"'.

Patricia Corbett, *Verdura: The Life and Work of a Master Jeweller* (2002)

The Palermo-born jeweler Duke Fulco di Verdura (1898–1978) was a unique talent and a darling of the gods. Born into the declining Sicilian aristocracy described in his cousin Prince Giuseppe di Lampedusa's novel *The Leopard* (1958), the handsome, amusing young socialite had the great fortune to meet the wealthy American composer Cole Porter and his wife, Linda, on the Lido in Venice in 1919. The Porters would become lifelong patrons, friends and backers. Through them, Verdura charmed the Parisian couturier Gabrielle 'Coco' Chanel, who employed him first as a textile designer and then as her jeweler.

Against a backdrop of costume parties and soirées at the Parisian club Le Grand Duc, where the cabaret star Bricktop [Ada Smith] taught Verdura and his glamorous chums Baron Nicolas de Gunzburg and Princess Natalia Paley the Charleston, Verdura developed a Byzantine sensibility, mixing precious and semi-precious stones, favouring cabochon-cut stones and settings of yellow gold. His coloured-stone Byzantine brooches (c.1930), inspired by the mosaics in the church of San Vitale, Ravenna, caught the eye of Diana Vreeland, then fashion editor of US *Harper's Bazaar* and ultimately the twentieth century's Empress of Fashion.

'Fulco was a real character and we adored him. He was unique, just like his

work,' said Vreeland, who was instrumental in introducing Verdura in New York when he, Baron de Gunzburg and the Princess Paley crossed the Atlantic to make their fortunes in 1934. After a brief spell drifting in Los Angeles, Verdura moved to Manhattan. There Vreeland introduced him to Paul Flato, who made audacious designs for the reigning movie queens Marlene Dietrich, Katharine Hepburn, Joan Crawford and Mae West.

While working under his own signature for Flato, Verdura created a whimsical novelty cufflink in 18ct yellow gold, christened Nuts & Bolts [still made today by Verdura], with a screw mechanism to hold the cuffs together. It is an amusing piece of Surrealism that anticipates his collaboration with Salvador Dalí in 1941.

Verdura's most famous design for Chanel, his bombé enamel Maltese Cross cuff bracelets set with multicoloured cabochons [1935], was made on a brief return to Paris. The cuffs that became synonymous with Mademoiselle Chanel were described by *Harper's Bazaar* in 1937 as 'not a stone, not a setting, not a colour match … no combination is too fantastic.'

'Fantastic' is an apt description for the most famous jewels that leapt from Verdura's imagination, such as his jeweled pomegranate brooches split open to

Above. A Verdura 18ct gold textured Medusa ring in the form of a coiled serpent with cabochon-ruby eyes.

Opposite. A Verdura Ravenna pendant brooch. This masterpiece, first made for Coco Chanel, is a mosaic of faceted rubies, blue sapphires, yellow sapphires and faceted multicoloured stones set in 18ct yellow gold (c.1930). Tailoring by Sir Tom Baker.

The Verdura yellow-gold Shell Case, made to celebrate Cole Porter's score for the Fred Astaire and Rita Hayworth musical *You'll Never Get Rich* (1941), with matching Shell cufflinks.

These Verdura 18ct yellow-gold Nuts & Bolts cufflinks were made in the 1930s, while Verdura was designing for Paul Flato.

reveal clusters of cabochon rubies. He set a pair of diamond and yellow-gold wings on an aquamarine pin; he frosted a shell brooch with white diamonds; he tied a 60ct aquamarine with ribbons and bow knots of diamonds. These pieces were set for Verdura's swans – Mona Bismarck, Babe Paley, the Duchess of Windsor, Slim Keith – but he did make for men, notably the Baron de Gunzburg (diamond-studded black-pearl cufflinks set in cages of thin yellow gold) and his best client, Cole Porter.

In 1936 Verdura was commissioned by Porter to make a jeweled cigarette case for Linda to celebrate the Broadway opening of his musical *Red Hot and Blue*. The Verdura for Flato platinum case was encrusted with rubies and sapphires dotted with white-diamond stars. At its centre was a white-diamond ray motif that could be detached and worn as a brooch. From then on, Linda would commission Verdura to design her husband's first-night

cigarette cases. It was Porter, with Viscount Astor, who financed Verdura's first atelier on Fifth Avenue in New York in 1939.

The Porter cigarette cases pushed Verdura to greater heights of ingenuity. The scalloped yellow-gold Shell Case, celebrating the Fred Astaire and Rita Hayworth film *You'll Never Get Rich* (1941), followed the contours of a clamshell. Feathers sculpted in gold inspired the box to mark the release of the film *Something to Shout About* in 1943. These cases are not only some of Verdura's finest work, but also rather poignant, since it was an open secret in Manhattan that the Porters' marriage was tinged with lavender.

Verdura's panama hat was the starting point for the cigarette case that commemorated the Broadway musical *Panama Hattie* (1940). The loose-weave yellow-gold technique was used to encase blue enamel for a cufflink that was bought by Gary Cooper and the Duke of Windsor.

Opposite. Verdura shows Coco Chanel his Maltese Cross bracelet in about 1935.

Above. This audacious 14ct rose-gold radiating-star brooch by Verdura with a central 8.35ct round brilliant-cut citrine (c.1941) was sold by Bonhams New York for $6,250 in 2017.

Left. Verdura Chevron Knot 18ct yellow-gold and black-enamel cufflinks.

The idea of a demi-parure – a set of matching jewels for a man – comprising cigarette case and cufflinks perfectly describes the sophistication of the Manhattan cafe-society years between the wars.

Verdura's most enduring cufflink design, Night & Day, was made for Cole Porter in 1941 and referred to one of his most poignant love songs, from *Gay Divorce* (1932). The lyric reads, 'Night and day, you are the one.' Verdura interpreted the line 'Only you beneath the moon and under the sun' by making irregular spherical enamel links: one dotted with diamonds to represent the night sky, the other a globe with continents described in yellow gold. The terminals of each link are a simple twisted bar. The design was adapted for a set of dress studs.

The *New York Times* christened Verdura 'America's Crown Jeweler', and the title has endured. The firm that bears his name has been owned since 1985 by former Sotheby's head of jewelry Ward Landrigan, whose son Nico has been president and CEO since 2003. The studio in Manhattan creates designs from a collection of more than 10,000 original sketches by Verdura. In 2014 the Landrigans celebrated the 75th anniversary of Verdura with an exhibition in the New York showroom, bringing together pieces from private and museum collections including Chanel's Maltese Cross cuffs, Greta Garbo's watch/bracelet and Porter cigarette cases.

www.verdura.com

Opposite. Originally made for Cole Porter in 1941 to celebrate his eponymous love song, Verdura's Night & Day cufflinks and dress studs are the house's most popular design for men. The links depict a globe and a night sky rendered in diamonds, enamel and 18ct yellow gold, with four Night dress studs.

Below. Verdura 18ct yellow-gold Log cufflinks.

CHAPTER FIVE

BRACELETS AND CUFFS

—

BRACELETS AND CUFFS

'Today what was a trend has matured into a staple. Taken as a whole, "Man Bling" encompasses not just bracelets but other forms of adornment, such as rings, tie clips and lapel pins – as well as longer-established accessories such as cufflinks and watches.'

Dan Rookwood, US editor of *Mr Porter* (2016)

In 2016 royal watchers confirmed that Prince Harry and his now wife, the Canadian actress Meghan Markle, were a serious item because both wore identical friendship bracelets. Prince Harry has worn beads and skeins of thread since his Eton days, but now the Meghan bracelet never leaves his wrist. It is a sign of the times that a British royal male wears beads that cost a few pounds, when his great-great-uncle the Duke of Windsor spent a decade between 1934 and 1944 collecting nine multicoloured gem-set Latin crosses, each inscribed with a billet-doux ('God Save the King for Wallis', for example) that Cartier set for the Duchess of Windsor. That bracelet sold at Sotheby's London in 2010 for £601,250.

Wearing multiple men's bracelets for sentiment's sake or fashion is so mainstream now for men of all ages that jewelers are looking to trade up on the trend and replace ethnic beads and threads with precious metal. Ceramics, such as Stephen Webster's England Made Me Cuban curb-link bracelet, form an interesting bridge, as does David Yurman's Chevron woven-rubber bracelet with an 18ct yellow-gold clasp. Shaun Leane was way ahead of the game when he designed a signature leather-and-diamond cuff in 2008. The Sabre is a thick band of black calf leather with ribbon-thin thongs that wind around the wrist, secured by a pavé-diamond tusk inspired by the jeweler's travels in South Africa.

Each of the fine jewelry houses has a signature yellow-gold bracelet design for men. For Boucheron it is the Quatre radiant edition in Grosgrain-pattern yellow gold with a line of pavé white diamonds. For Tiffany & Co. it is a clever yellow-gold bracelet with T-motif links, and for Cartier it is the Santos de Cartier yellow-gold and steel belcher chain link. Although he is a mighty goldsmith where chains are concerned, one of Webster's purest bracelet designs is the yellow-gold I Promise to Love You neon bangle, a collaboration with his friend the artist Tracey Emin, calibré-set with rubies and inscribed within the band in Emin's hand. Leane's 18ct white-gold scaled thirty-three-link Serpent bracelet (page 186) is a unique interpretation of a familiar inspiration. David Yurman's is the classic 18ct yellow-gold Cable cuff, and Theo Fennell's

Page 182. The actor Chris Hemsworth photographed in Los Angeles in 2016 wearing carved silver tube rings and bracelet designed by the Israeli-born, Los Angeles-based cult men's jeweler M. Cohen.

Above. A Cartier Santos de Cartier 18ct yellow-gold anchor-link bracelet.

Opposite. The actor Marlon Brando on the set of the film *A Streetcar Named Desire* (1951) wearing his personally owned silver ID bracelet as the anti-hero Stanley Kowalski.

'The 1940s school of polished yellow-gold mechanical bracelets epitomized by Cartier's Tank Tracks and Bicycle Chain links echo industrialization and have the gravitas to sit handsomely on a man's arm.'

Above. An art deco square-diamond line bracelet from Hancocks, mounted in engraved platinum (c.1930).

Opposite, top. The Shaun Leane 18ct white-gold and diamond thirty-three-link Serpent bracelet with 3.94ct of white diamonds.

Opposite, bottom. A trio of Boucheron Quatre Grosgrain bracelets in 18ct white, yellow and rose gold.

18ct yellow-gold palmier (rope-twist) chain bracelet with a hand terminal is as finely balanced a chain as you will find in modern jewelry.

Unlike with stick pins or dress sets, contemporary jewelers are investing heavily in the men's bracelet, safe in the knowledge that supply is scarce at the antique and auction end of the market. With few exceptions, antique fine-jewelry bracelets are problematic for men. There is little chance that a period bracelet set for women will fit a man's wrist, and alteration destroys the value of a signed piece. Stylistically, bejeweled antique bracelets of any era are too dainty. These jewels were largely showpieces worn on a lady's bare or gloved wrist, and were not designed to sit uncomfortably and half-concealed beneath a man's shirt cuff. Even in this age of gender fluidity, a Cartier Tutti Frutti, Bulgari Serpenti or Elsa Peretti for Tiffany & Co. Bone cuff is not designed in proportion to be worn on a man's arm, although the new Peretti Bone, with a black finish over copper, has promise.

The exceptions come, as exceptions invariably do, from Cartier's workshops above the original flagship on Rue de la Paix in Paris. The 1940s school of polished yellow-gold mechanical bracelets epitomized by Cartier's 'tank track' and 'bicycle chain' links echo industrialization and have the gravitas to sit handsomely on a man's arm. Similarly, the two Cartier superstar Juste un Clou and Love bracelets from the 1970s in yellow, white or rose gold are such pure designs that they suit both sexes, with or without diamond embellishment. A yellow-gold and white pavé-diamond Juste un Clou looked particularly sharp when worn by Lewis Hamilton at the *Time* 100 Gala in New York in 2016. Where Hamilton leads, his young male fans will inevitably follow – where they have sufficient funds.

In the early 1940s Fulco di Verdura designed a yellow-gold curb-link watch bracelet that was worn by the Swedish screen goddess Greta Garbo. Garbo was famed for introducing tailored men's trousers to Hollywood in the 1930s, and she favoured robust, masculine jewelry. Unsurprisingly, Verdura's gold curb-link bracelets became popular with men of fashion, such as Noël Coward. A Verdura double-rope-twist curb-link bracelet, watch and ring sold at Bonhams in 2016 for £14,375. Among the auction

'The auction houses and antiques dealers are worth plundering for the very simplest diamond, emerald, ruby or sapphire line bracelets that were hugely popular in the 1920s and 1930s.'

results from all the big houses in London, New York, Geneva and Hong Kong, the dearth of fine jewelry bracelets for men is striking. The exception is Bonhams' 'Rare Jewels and Jadeite' sales, where milky-green jade men's bangles invariably come up. A jadeite bangle sold at Bonhams Hong Kong in 2016 realized £67,000 – clearly not a fashion or impulse purchase.

Although the twentieth-century style idols such as Garbo, Nancy Cunard and Diana Vreeland may have enjoyed the dramatic chink of multiple precious metal or jade bracelets and bangles, it is only men such as Johnny Depp, Steven Tyler and Keith Richards who stack their wrists with beads and heavy metal. A precious metal bracelet should have weight but also be pleasing and comfortable to wear. Wright & Teague's Iliad cuff (see page 245), a medium band of gently undulating yellow gold, bends to the wrist for a secure fit. One of their most unusual pieces of jewelry is the 18ct yellow-gold Mystic bracelet, each bean-shaped bead pressed with the imprints of the designers' fingers. The bracelet is as satisfying to handle as a rope of Greek worry beads and is cast in silver and white, yellow and rose gold.

Hamilton has proved that a gem-set bracelet is a frontier that has been crossed, just as the solitaire diamond earring for men is now far from uncommon. The auction houses and antiques dealers are worth plundering for the very simplest diamond, emerald, ruby or sapphire line bracelets that were hugely popular in the 1920s and 1930s. The hip-hop mmunity has already embraced the diamond bracelet: Sean 'P. Diddy' Combs rocked an art deco white-diamond bracelet at the Beverly Hills Hotel back in 2004. A sliver of gemstones in a line bracelet is less bombastic, such as the brilliant-cut line bracelet that sold at Sotheby's in 2016 for £12,500, from a high estimate of £5,000. Sotheby's New York sold a set of line bracelets – one square-cut diamond, one step-cut emerald, one step-cut ruby and one step-cut sapphire – in 2016 for $43,750.

Contemporary jewelers are far from squeamish about setting men's bracelets and bangles with jewels. Stephen Webster upscaled his Shark Jaw white-gold and diamond ring (see page 95) into a cuff with jaws that snap around the wrist, set with white-diamond fangs. Shaun Leane has set his Serpent bracelet in white gold, sprinkling the scales with 3.94ct of

Above. Wright & Teague's Mystic bracelet – the marque's most popular bracelet design ever – in 18ct yellow gold and sterling silver.

Opposite. Magnificent heavy platinum Verdura curb-link bracelets that snap into a single chain collar (c.1980). Courtesy of Hancocks.

Overleaf. A Theo Fennell 18ct yellow-gold, diamond and ruby Snake bracelet with handmade palmier chain.

Above. A Shaun Leane
magnetized gold-vermeil
and leather-thong bracelet.

Opposite. The actor Clark Gable
wears a yellow-gold anchor-link
bracelet inscribed 'I LOVE YOU,
CL' on the back. It was a gift in
1934 from his mistress Carole
Lombard, whom he would marry
in 1939.

Below. A sterling silver interlocking
bangle by Shaun Leane.

pavé-set diamonds, which have strength and menace. Theo Fennell's torc bangle in white gold has skull and snake terminals embellished with black diamonds, but his most successful bracelet design for men is an 18ct yellow-gold, diamond and ruby snake with the handmade palmier-chain body and the snake's head biting its tail to complete the circle. Solange Azagury-Partridge's blackened-gold writhing Snake bangle, set with diamond eyes, looks as though it was excavated from a tomb in the Valley of the Kings (see page 86).

The bracelet or bangle as a symbol of commitment and/or ownership is as old as civilization itself. The British Museum has a fine Persian example in yellow gold from the Oxus Treasure, dating from the fifth century BC, with twists of gold locking around the wrist and terminals shaped like snake heads. Azagury-Partridge is well-versed in the language of jewelry, and has created two simply beautiful pieces for men: a blackened 18ct yellow-gold Love Knot bangle and a bracelet crafted from blackened-gold chain link, made to order with a lock of one's lover's hair (see page 85).

Cartier's Love bracelet, set with lockable screws and sold with a screwdriver, was designed by Aldo Cipullo in 1969 and first worn by Elizabeth Taylor and Richard Burton. Of his chastity-belt-inspired design, Cipullo said: 'What modern people want are love symbols that look semi-permanent – or at least require a trick to remove. After all, love symbols should suggest an everlasting quality.' The bracelet has achieved cult status among Millennials thanks to Kanye West, Kim Kardashian, Kylie Jenner and Justin Bieber. Bieber posts endless images of his white-diamond-set Love and Juste un Clou bracelets.

If one looks back beyond the 1970s, when the chunky yellow-gold bracelet started to be associated with the pawnbroker's shop window and sovereign rings, the role models grow in stature. One of the great romances in 1930s Hollywood can be dated from a photograph from 1934 of Clark Gable wearing a yellow-gold anchor-link bracelet. The *Gone with the Wind* idol's initials are inscribed on the plate, with 'I LOVE YOU, CL' on the reverse. Gable was still married to Ria Franklin, but had begun an affair with the love of his life, Carole Lombard. They would marry in 1939, only for Lombard to die in a plane crash three years later. The love token

Above. A Cartier 18ct white-gold Juste un Clou bracelet set with pavé diamonds.

Opposite. The actor Paul Newman wears a yellow-gold ID bracelet in the film *Sweet Bird of Youth* (1962).

was sold at Christie's New York in 2006 for $7,800. A gold medical ID bracelet inscribed with Gable's medical number and blood group sold in 2010 for $5,000.

Dog-tag chains and ID bracelets worn by the US military during the Second World War became fashionable, masculine pieces of jewelry in the 1950s, as worn by the new generation of method actors Marlon Brando, James Dean and Montgomery Clift. Brando most famously wore a gold ID bracelet playing thuggish, tortured Stanley Kowalski in the film adaptation of Tennessee Williams's *A Streetcar Named Desire* (1951). His lifelong friend and rumoured lover Wally Cox, with whose ashes Brando's were scattered, gave Williams a silver ID bracelet. The bisexual *Rebel Without a Cause* star James Dean's sterling silver ID bracelet was inscribed JAMES, with DD 1955 on the reverse of the plate. DD stood for Dilemma Dean, and 1955 was the year of the twenty-four-year-old actor's fatal car crash in his Porsche Spyder, nicknamed 'Little Bastard'. The bracelet was auctioned by Guernsey's in 2011 with an estimate of $20,000–30,000.

Elvis Presley seemed to give gold ID bracelets to fans, groupies and security guards the way tennis players throw sweat bands. He wore the most identifiable – a yellow-gold curb-link with ELVIS spelled out in forty-eight diamonds – at his Las Vegas comeback in 1969 and his 'white-rhinestone flared jumpsuit' television special recorded in Hawaii in 1973. He gave the piece to his fiancée Ginger Alden in 1978, and she sold it at auction in 2010 for an estimated $400,000–500,000. A woven roped yellow-gold-mesh ID bracelet Presley gave to a girlfriend was sold at Graceland for $27,000, after a high estimate of $10,000. Yet another unusual yellow-gold sash bracelet, made from twin-row rope chains linked to a central textured barrel terminal with woven articulated tassels, was given by Presley to a security guard at a concert in Cincinnati; Julien's Auctions in Los Angeles sold it in 2015 for $10,880. Modern Hollywood men who have upped their game to sterling silver or yellow-gold chain-link bracelets include Michael Fassbender, Channing Tatum, Guy Pearce, Elijah Kelley, Jeremy Piven and Sean Pertwee.

BENTLEY & SKINNER

'The gentleman who buys fine jewelry at Bentley & Skinner
has a passion for collecting. If a piece speaks to him, the
decision is made on the spot.'

Mark Evans, chairman, Bentley & Skinner

It was a stroke of genius for Bentley &
Skinner to quit New Bond Street in 2010
for large new premises at 55 Piccadilly.
New Bond Street, which *Vogue* jewelry
editor Carol Woolton calls 'the diamond
dash', has the highest concentration of
magnificent jewelry of any street in the
world, and blinds the passer-by with an
embarrassment of riches. By contrast,
Bentley & Skinner stands alone on
Piccadilly, with vast sheet-glass windows
of gargantuan wingspan, within which
is a history of grand jewelry design from
the Georgian period to the present.

Bentley & Skinner 'has been selling
the loveliest jewelry since 1880', in its
own words, latterly under the auspices
of chairman and Royal Warrant holder
Mark Evans and salesman Omar Vaja.
The windows literally stop traffic: one entire
tier is dedicated to rare diamond tiaras
that escaped being broken up largely
because they are set to be converted into
necklaces, brooches and dress clips. Every
permutation of diamond and gem-set
brooch, from Edwardian dragonflies set
en tremblant to jazzy diamond, emerald
and onyx jabot pins, is on display next to
natural-pearl chokers, Fabergé stick pins
and Victorian diamond collet necklaces.

Other antique jewelers may show a
token cufflink in their window, but Bentley
& Skinner has a bravura display of precious
novelty links united only by sheer artistry.

Dice links are far from uncommon. However,
in the hands of Cartier's workshops circa
1955 two three-dimensional cross-etched
yellow-gold dice set with round brilliant-cut
diamonds make the cleverest *trompe l'œil*
chain links (see page 72). All the important
marques are present: a Boucheron 18ct
yellow-gold and square-cut cabochon-
sapphire stirrup cufflink (c.1935) (see page
119), a Mellerio yellow-gold hunting-horn
cufflink (1900) and a perfect marquise-
shaped Fabergé white-enamel and
rose-cut diamond link (1890).

'We do have a few collectors who have
a great love of antique jewelry for men ...
particularly cufflinks,' says Evans. 'One of
our best customers had easily more than
100 pairs of fine antique cufflinks in an
extraordinary collection that ought to be in
a museum. Interestingly, he was incredibly
knowledgeable about the history of jewelry
but he bought on a purely instinctive level.
When he'd seen something out of the
corner of his eye that spoke to him, the only
thing he questioned was the price. Another
of our male clients had a passion for very
large jeweled brooches. Nothing he bought
was signed. He was more interested in the
appearance: the bigger the better, as it
happens. His collection was to be worn
and enjoyed.'

Evans is one of the few antique jewelers
in London – if not the world – with a
workshop that can create ingenious pieces

Above. A late nineteenth-century
garnet-and-diamond beetle
brooch (1890).

Opposite. A 22ct yellow-gold
bee brooch with fine twisted
wirework circles and stripes
on the thorax and abdomen.
Hallmarked London 2012,
bearing the Bentley & Skinner
sponsor mark. Tailoring by
Turnbull & Asser.

of men's dress jewelry in the grand tradition, such as a tortoise-motif dress set described in round- and baguette-cut diamonds or 18ct yellow-gold castings of animal stick pins from a collection of 1930s emblems, such as running foxes, corgis, bulldogs and greyhounds. He dreamed up an 18ct yellow-gold galleon brooch setting for a 21.53ct boulder opal that was set in the hull of the ship, and he stocks a collection of intricate twisted 18ct yellow-gold wirework bee brooches by the contemporary Italian jeweler Gaetano Chiavetta.

The workshop is invaluable not only for giving first aid to neglected antique jewels but also for framing acquisitions, such as a Regency cameo (c.1810) that was set as an 18ct yellow-gold stick pin or a Roman carnelian intaglio in a yellow-gold signet-ring mount. 'Intaglios and cameos are glorious things whether they are Roman, Renaissance, Regency or Victorian,' says Evans, 'but we tend to have more interest from American men. Englishmen tend to be shy about jewelry, but this is changing. A gentleman came in recently looking at our skull diamond rings as a gift for his wife and walked out having left an order for a stick pin for himself instead.'

When questioned about investing in jewelry, Vaja looks slightly pained: 'You've got to love the piece. If it is a thing of beauty, beautifully made, and you've amassed enough good-quality pieces, the collection will inevitably be worth a lot of money.' Both Evans and Vaja earmark antique brooches as a burgeoning market for men's dress jewelry. As Evans says, 'On Bond Street in 1973 ... men still wore bowler hats and red carnations in their buttonholes. That's all gone now, but it leaves a space on the man's lapel for a brooch or pin that delights the eye.'

Bentley & Skinner's path to 55 Piccadilly has more twists and turns than the coast road to Monte Carlo. A. E. Skinner & Co. (founded 1880) was jeweler by Royal Appointment to Queen Victoria, and took up residence at 34–35 New Bond Street (now Sotheby's) in 1922, bearing the crests of King George V and his magpie consort, Queen Mary. Bentley & Co. (founded early 1920s) was a Bond Street neighbour at no. 65, and was bought by the present chairman's uncle John Sheldon in 1934. Sheldon was swift to save Georgian and Victorian jewels imperilled by the 1920s fashion for art deco settings. Evans, who joined his uncle's firm in 1973, moved Bentley & Co. to 8 New Bond Street in 1992 and merged the company with Skinner & Co. in 1998. In 2010, after

Above. Victorian snake figure-of-eight brooch set with eight-cut diamonds, ruby eyes and suspending a diamond-and-natural-pearl drop (c.1870).

Below. A Victorian diamond pheasant brooch pavé set with rose-cut diamonds with a cabochon-ruby eye (c.1880).

Left. Art nouveau yellow-gold, enamel and brilliant-cut-diamond Mythical Creature cufflinks (1895).

a brief hiatus in reduced circumstances in the Burlington Arcade, Bentley & Skinner moved to its magnificent new premises on Piccadilly, opposite Fortnum & Mason. There, in addition to the blaze of tiaras in the window, Evans put in a street-view window looking in on his workshops. He is Royal Warrant holder for HM The Queen and HRH The Prince of Wales.

The shop on Piccadilly has proved to be an ideal home for the firm, since it has not only a vast ground-floor salon but also a gallery below for the firm's considerable selling collection of Fabergé. 'It is often the men whose eyes are arrested by our windows,' says Vaja. 'Some of the chaps are more enthusiastic than the wives or partners for whom the jewels are being purchased. Fortunately, we have pieces of gentlemen's jewelry that might satisfy their curiosity.'

www.bentley-skinner.com

Opposite. A French art deco diamond-and-carved-emerald brooch in the form of a stylized bay tree comprising openwork diamond-set foliage, claw-set carved-emerald flowers, a black-enamel stem and an openwork planter set with brilliant- and baguette-cut diamonds (c.1920). Tailoring by Turnbull & Asser.

Left. Fabergé ruby-and-enamel cufflinks set with the Russian imperial crown in cabochon rubies and rose-cut diamonds (c.1890).

HANCOCKS

'It doesn't go without notice at Hancocks that in many cases the gentleman is much more interested and informed about antique jewelry than the lady. You can see the switch has been clicked and that the desire for the jewel is being led by the man.'

Guy Burton

Hancocks has set and sold antique and contemporary jewelry in London's West End since 1849. In 1856 its founder, Charles Frederick Hancock, created his masterpiece for the 6th 'Bachelor' Duke of Devonshire, William Cavendish: a magnificent seven-piece parure of antique and Renaissance cameos and intaglios carved from multicoloured precious and hardstones set in yellow gold with rich enamel decoration. The jewels were worn by Lady Grenville at the coronation of Tsar Alexander II of Russia, and remain in the Chatsworth collection. The parure, resembling medieval crown jewels, was one of the most influential jewelry designs of the Victorian era.

An enduring appreciation of exceptional design and make endures at Hancocks to the present day. Now trading in the Burlington Arcade under the guardianship of Stephen and Janie Burton, Hancocks is a truly rounded jewelry firm. The couple's daughter Amy Burton is both an instinctively strong buyer of antique jewelry and a talented designer of contemporary fine jewelry. Their son Guy is a connoisseur of old-cut diamonds and director of Hancocks' bespoke service, and oversees the company's roaring trade in signet rings. The treasures in the window are the best examples from the golden eras of old master jewelers such as Wiese, LaCloche Frères, Pierre Sterlé, Cartier, Buccellati, Boivin, Verdura and Andrew Grima.

The Burlington Arcade is a magnet for gentlemen who appreciate the beauty and rarity of a 1930s diamond-and-sapphire dress set sparkling seductively in Hancocks' window. 'It is increasingly hard to find a complete dress set,' says Guy Burton, 'and even harder to find one signed by Cartier, LaCloche or Van Cleef & Arpels. We have three lovely dress sets at the moment, but that's deceptive. In the last five years we might have found only seven or eight top-quality sets. We never let a superb dress set pass, because they are in high demand. ... Provenance is very important to our customers. When we know the stories it is gold dust, but even if we don't, you and I know that a really handsome gem-set cufflink or dress set acquired at Cartier or Boucheron will have seen some very special evenings. Men in particular love the history of jewels and gemstones. There is a definite connection with a more elegant age of jewelry for gentlemen.' He shows off an 18ct yellow-gold Cartier dress set from 1935, inlaid with engine-turned white-gold discs, outlined in black enamel and centred with brilliant-cut diamonds in black-onyx collars.

In addition to collectible dress sets and cufflinks, such as a delicate LaCloche Frères hexagonal platinum-and-diamond honeycomb design from c.1925 [see page 67], Hancocks is a trusted source of men's

A Van Cleef & Arpels textured 18ct yellow-gold elephant brooch with emerald-set eyes, white-agate tusks and black-enamel feet. Tailoring by Henry Poole & Co.

'We are the oldest family-owned jeweler in London, which might explain why the family ring is such a cornerstone of the business.'

Guy Burton

Above. An 18ct yellow-gold, Burmese ruby and old mine cushion-cut-diamond dress ring (c.1945) by Boucheron.

Opposite. A meticulously detailed bee brooch (c.1880) crafted with a cabochon tiger's eye, diamonds and enamel set in silver and gold. Tailoring by Henry Poole & Co.

right-hand rings, such as a sinuous 18ct yellow-gold example from Boucheron (c.1945) set with a Burmese ruby and an old-cut diamond. Burton's knowledge of old cuts and his identification of untreated precious stones is reassuring, to say the least, when a jewel might carry a five-figure price ticket. 'Interestingly, a lot of mid-twentieth-century designs for rings have a masculine draw, as do Andrew Grima's rings from the 1970s. Buccellati rings are completely unisex. We have a lot of gentlemen trying Grima rings: they are such strong, graphic designs around extraordinary gemstones.'

The majority of British men still don't wear wedding rings, but orders for Hancocks-designed classic Oxford oval signet rings carved with a family crest or initials are reaching six or seven a week, with a bias towards solid white, rose or yellow gold rather than intaglio hardstone settings. 'We are the oldest family-owned jeweler in London, which might explain why the family ring is such a cornerstone of the business,' says Burton. 'As for fancier rings, we tend to find that good design appeals equally to men and women. A lot of Amy's work applies to men, particularly her Disorient ring. Disorient is such a strong, architectural design and each ring is handmade for each customer, so there is no question of having to resize.'

Guy Burton's passion for old-cut diamonds set in the contemporary collection makes a modern Hancocks engagement or right-hand ring a much more subtle proposition for men. Whereas modern-cut diamonds sparkle like electric light, the old cuts shimmer like candlelight. So when Hancocks sets a platinum full eternity ring with 4.9ct of old European-cut diamonds, the result is a smoulder rather than a lightning flash, and it looks entirely appropriate on a man's hand. The platinum fine twist ring set with round brilliant-cut diamonds shows impeccable workmanship, the metal and stones in perfect balance. 'I'm sure you're not hearing this for the first time,' Burton explains, 'but in a lot of cases the gentleman is more interested than the lady when they come in to buy a diamond engagement ring or a brooch. In fact, the real surprise for us is the popularity of antique brooches bought by men and for men. We had a lovely 1950s Cartier wirework dog brooch with an articulated head and ruby eyes that was bought for a man. You can imagine our Pierre Sterlé c.1950 gold leaf brooches (see page 154) scattered with round brilliant-cut diamonds would work rather well on a lapel, as would our Lalique enamel brooch.'

Hancocks' men's jewelry trade is largely European-American, but momentum is growing among Middle Eastern, Indian and

Far Eastern customers. 'The interesting thing about meeting international clients is that you discover a new jewelry superstition and learn every day,' Burton says. 'With the exception of jadeite, traditionally the Chinese don't buy antique jewelry because of the karma relating to previous owners, but the business is getting more interesting when we go on our Hong Kong trips, for example. Indian men are naturally drawn to Cartier's Tutti Frutti settings of carved coloured gemstones, because their culture inspired the design in the early twentieth century.'

In addition to the popularity of brooches for men, Burton has noticed an appetite for substantial 1940s–1960s 18ct yellow-gold bracelets, such as an unsigned 1940s American example with Oldsmobile car-shaped links between two rows of baton links, and a 1950s tyre-track motif by Cartier. 'More men than women try on our yellow-gold bracelets,' he says, 'and whereas once only interest was shown, now men are increasingly committed to follow up and buy the piece of jewelry.'

www.hancocks-london.com

Left. The contemporary Disorient ring by Amy Burton, in 18ct yellow gold with a round brilliant-cut diamond in openwork sculptural design. Tailoring by Turnbull & Asser.

Opposite. A contemporary white-gold, freshwater-pearl, black-diamond and white-diamond spider brooch by E. Wolfe & Co. with cabochon-ruby eyes and white-gold fangs. Tailoring by Henry Poole & Co.

WARTSKI

'You can't sell anything to anybody ever. You can only articulate what is wonderful about a particular piece. If you do that, then you're a good salesman.'

Geoffrey Munn

Despite the fact that the company has been in London since 1911, its sign still reads 'Wartski of Llandudno'. It is a reference to the firm's founder, the Polish peddler Morris Wartski, who, under the patronage of the cross-dressing 5th Marquess of Anglesey, established in Bangor in 1865 the antique jeweler that would serve six successive British monarchs. Today Wartski is a league of extraordinary ladies and gentlemen led by the founder's maternal great-grandson Nicholas Snowman and managing director Geoffrey Munn, who is treasure-hunter-in-chief to the BBC's *Antiques Roadshow* and a world authority on Fabergé.

On any given day one can find Munn (who joined Wartski in 1972) rhapsodizing beneath a portrait of Queen Alexandra about house treasures, such as the aquamarine Fabergé brooch that Kenneth Snowman (Nicholas's father) acquired and director Katherine Purcell identified as an engagement present from Tsar Nicholas II to Empress Alexandra. Director Kieran McCarthy may recount the story of his 'Lost Arc' moment, when an American dealer appeared with an 8-centimetre (3¼-inch) gold, blue-sapphire and diamond egg containing a Vacheron Constantin watch that he'd paid £8,000 for in a flea market. It proved to be one of the eight lost Fabergé imperial Easter eggs, a gift to Empress Maria Feodorovna from her

husband, Tsar Alexander III, in 1887. The divine folly sold in 2014 for a reported £20 million.

The firm's gallery executive Thomas Holman, the youngest of its extraordinary gentlemen, has a particular interest in jewelry for men, specifically jeweled stick pins, and his knowledge is encyclopaedic. Like Munn, Holman believes that in order to get into Wartski, objects must be little works of art in their own right. Holding a gem-set Cartier stick pin with a peacock-feather motif (c.1920), he says, 'jeweled pins have a fascination for men not least because of the ingenuity of setting an amusing design in such small scale.'

Holman's eyes sparkle as he describes rare electric jewels set by Auguste-Germain Cadet-Picard in the 1860s and wired with a miniature battery patented by Gustave Trouvé in 1865. Cadet-Picard's gold-and-enamel skull stick pin of 1867 (now in the Victoria and Albert Museum) was made with hinged jaws that snapped open and shut, the battery connected invisibly by wire. 'They were described as jewels of near-terrifying originality,' says Holman of automaton stick pins made in the style of drumming monkeys, hummingbirds in flight, butterflies and dancing Harlequins. 'Cadet-Picard stick pins in working order are incredibly rare.'

As chronicled in Munn's *Wartski: The First Hundred and Fifty Years* (2015), the

Above. An English yellow-gold Beetle brooch set with demantoid garnets and diamonds (c.1900).

Opposite. A platinum-and-diamond brooch with ruby, sapphire, citrine and amethyst flowers, each flower centred with a diamond in an arched diamond frame (c.1935). The five articulated drops suspending pear-shaped diamonds can be removed. Tailoring by Turnbull & Asser.

'The thing about some of these objects is that they're like one's friends ...
they're completely charming and sometimes utterly useless.'
Geoffrey Munn

Opposite. A platinum-and-diamond brooch modelled as an upturned openwork urn with calibré- and brilliant-cut diamonds pouring out of it (c.1910). The brilliant-cut diamonds are articulated and sparkle like falling water. Tailoring by Henry Poole & Co.

Below. An art deco diamond-and-rock-crystal clip. The pure white rock crystal is carved into an architectural scroll and highlighted with a raised, curved and tapering band of brilliant-cut diamonds.

company's fortunes were made in 1927 when its owner, Emanuel Snowman, took £100,000 to the Soviet Union and acquired eighty pieces confiscated from the imperial family, including nine Fabergé eggs. Snowman's son Kenneth, a friend of the James Bond author Ian Fleming, appears as himself in Fleming's short story 'The Property of a Lady' (1963), and Wartski had a cameo role in the 007 film *Octopussy* (1983), the plot of which turns on an imperial Easter egg. The affable Kenneth was responsible for bringing some of the firm's most influential male clients to Grafton Street, including Yul Brynner, Bing Crosby, Frank Sinatra and John F. Kennedy, who bought his First Lady, Jackie, her famous diamond sunburst hair ornament there.

Surveying displays containing Fabergé guilloché and gem-set picture frames, a carved-nephrite-and-gold paper knife (1899), agate and diamond animal novelties (1890) and silver-gilt, enamel and sapphire cigarette cases, Munn says: 'The thing about some of these objects is that they're like one's friends. . .they're completely charming and sometimes utterly useless.' For collectors, an enamel-and-diamond Fabergé paperclip from 1911 sums up the causes of the Russian Revolution in just one inconsequential, elaborate object. Holman produces a pair of Fabergé cufflinks (1896–1908) as if they were a favourite godchild. The exquisite

links comprise four reeded platinum balls surmounted by cabochon star sapphires, peppered with rose-cut diamonds and joined by yellow-gold curb-link chains.

The emotion invested in buying jewelry for Wartski is matched by a thirst for imparting knowledge that goes far beyond retail. Holman shows a rare-as-hen's-teeth yellow-gold pentagonal four-terminal Giuliano cufflink made in about 1880. The terminals are cast and chased to depict a helmeted warrior, possibly Achilles. Wartski's research in the British Museum identified the ancient intaglio gold ring from which Giuliano cast a plaster impression. Wartski's library of jewelry monographs is impressive. Munn has written countless books, though none as popular as *Tiaras: A History of Splendour*, published to coincide with the V&A exhibition he curated in 2002. Purcell wrote *Falize: A Dynasty of Jewellers* (1999) and McCarthy *Fabergé in London: The British Branch of the Imperial Russian Goldsmith* (2017). The late chairman, Kenneth Snowman, was a prolific writer on Fabergé and other famous marques.

Munn is particularly charismatic on television because he communicates histories as intricate as the jewels he assesses with a lightness of touch and an evident delight in his subject. What first appears to be a chic little art deco Cartier cufflink set with onyx and diamonds comes

to life when he reveals that the link dates from 1920 and was one of Charles Jacqueau's first series of Panthère de Cartier designs for men, and adds that Cartier's artistic advisor Jeanne Toussaint was nicknamed 'Panther'. Holman is equally adept at answering questions of attribution, although he is swift to point out that an unsigned gem-set target stick pin, for example, is likely to have been made in the same Parisian workshop as those sold by Cartier, Van Cleef & Arpels and Boucheron.

In addition to a Fabergé collection unsurpassed in London, Wartski sells masterpieces worthy of a maharaja and signed by the royal family of historic jewel houses: an extravagant Van Cleef & Arpels diamond feather brooch (1928), an impressive Tiffany & Co. emerald briolette stick pin entwined by diamond-set snakes (1900) (see page 102), a LaCloche Frères geometric art deco diamond pin (c.1930), a Paul Flato yellow-gold 'money-bag'

brooch peppered with diamonds, sapphires and rubies (c.1942), and an exceptional neo-Egyptian yellow-gold pharaoh's-head brooch made by John Brogden in 1870.

Demand for gentlemen's jewelry is also reflected in the small collection of pieces made in the antique style by Wartski's workshop, such as 18ct yellow-gold cabochon red-garnet four-terminal cufflinks and a marvellous Crab pin pavé-set with 5.9ct of brilliant-cut diamonds. Wartski made the wedding rings for the Prince of Wales and the Duchess of Cornwall in 2005, and for the Duchess of Cambridge in 2011, from Welsh gold given to them by the Queen. The firm also holds the Royal Warrants of HM The Queen and HRH The Prince of Wales.

'Having been at Wartski for over forty years, I've seen enormous peaks and troughs of wealth,' says Munn of the flotsam and jetsam of Russian, Gulf State, Chinese and Indian money that finds its

'The gentlemen who buy jewels at Wartski are becoming more adventurous in their choices. We have noticed an interest in gem-set brooches and the stick pin worn in the gentleman's jacket lapel.'

Thomas Holman

way to London's antique jewelers. 'Our patron saint, the 5th Marquess of Anglesey, bankrupted himself to the tune of £50 million in today's currency, had to auction the jewels he acquired at Wartski and died aged twenty-nine in Monte Carlo in 1905. So it would be rather amusing if men began to buy sumptuous jewels for themselves like our Dancing Marquess.' 'The gentlemen who buy jewels at Wartski are becoming more adventurous in their choices,' says Holman. 'We have noticed an interest in gem-set brooches and the stick pin worn in the gentleman's jacket lapel.' If you were in any doubt that Wartski considers the jewels and *objets d'art* it sells as works of art, Munn will remind you that Leonardo da Vinci, Hans Holbein the Younger, Albrecht Dürer and Nicholas Hilliard were all trained goldsmiths.

www.wartski.com

Left. A Wartski Crab brooch finely depicted in platinum and pavé set with 5.9ct of brilliant-cut diamonds.

Opposite. A LaCloche Frères brooch (c.1930) in the form of a platinum cylinder set with brilliant-cut diamonds, orbited by three extended diamond-set bands, with a row of square-cut diamonds running down the centre.

CHAPTER SIX

CHAINS AND PENDANTS

—

CHAINS AND PENDANTS

'The protective energy of the colour black is even more powerful in a diamond, the unscratchable stone. Its powers are maximized in the inverted setting, echoing defence spikes and directing the energy to flow outwards.'

Ara Vartanian

The talismanic nature of jewelry is best exemplified in the amulet pendant symbolically worn over the heart. The most common symbols are religious: the cross, the Jewish star, the Islamic crescent and star, the Buddhist Dharma wheel and the Hindu Om, all of which Solange Azagury-Partridge rendered in blackened 18ct yellow gold for her Love Thy Neighbour pendants in the 'Alpha' collection. Symbols such as the all-seeing eye have multilayered meanings associating them with ancient Egypt, the Freemasons and the Illuminati.

The Brazilian jeweler Ara Vartanian wears his own black rhodium-plated silver seven-point circular amulet pendant set with inverted black diamonds (see page 36) firm in the belief that the pyramid of the stone repels negativity and threat. It is one of three. 'It is an energy piece,' he says. 'Rolling Stones guitarist Ronnie Wood had come to my showroom in Brazil and bought quite a few pieces. I couldn't sell him the pendant because it was special to me so I gave it to him. He really believes in it as an amulet, and never takes it off. I gave Kate [Moss] the second one, made myself a third and that's it. That's where the energy circle closes.'

What distinguishes all the male jewelry designers interviewed for this book is the sheer volume of their own pieces that they wear with casual ease. Whether gay or straight, these men seem to absorb gemstones into their identity, and are their own best advertisements. Vartanian believes sexuality is 'a boring distinction. I have gay customers who wear the same pieces that I do. Who gives a s***? Jewelry is for whoever wants to wear it.' On the day we meet, in addition to the amulet pendant Vartanian puts on a necklace from his collaboration with Moss: a leather thong pendant half-set with black-diamond beads. It is one of the coolest pieces of modern men's jewelry, and is up there with Elsa Peretti's Diamonds by the Yard as a minimalist masterpiece. Stephen Webster, Shaun Leane, Theo Fennell and David Yurman's son and creative director Evan all wear pendants the way a Wall Street financier would a tie.

'Jewelry always started with the form, and almost all the shapes that we use in modern jewelry stem from ancient jewelry,' Evan Yurman told US *Esquire* in 2009. 'The key to all jewelry is in the ancients.' But it is the

Page 216. The actor Aldis Hodge attends the Academy Awards in 2017 wearing a sterling silver and jet lapel chain.

Above. The Theo Fennell Skeleton Key pendant made from 18ct white gold and pavé black and white diamonds. The snake eye is set with a cabochon ruby.

Opposite. The actor Steve McQueen exercises at Paramount Studios, Hollywood, in 1936, wearing the 14ct gold St Christopher given to him by his wife, Neile Adams.

jeweler's task to interpret ancient symbols from his or her own point of view. One of the cleverest Yurman pendants is a large sterling silver box chain that incorporates a black-diamond pavé-set cross horizontally within the chain, rather than hanging from it. Fennell has more cross-and-key pendants in his collection than the Vatican, making each new design and stone combination eminently collectible. His 18ct white-gold cross pavé-set with sapphires and entwined with a ribbon of white diamonds is a beauty, as is the amusing Skeleton Key design in 18ct white gold, black diamonds and rubies.

Although a young David Beckham wore multiple diamond crosses larger than the altarpiece of Santiago di Compostela, and Kanye West tried to break the world record for yellow-gold chains before his knees buckled under the weight, younger stars such as Channing Tatum and Ryan Gosling are mismatching pendants that have meaning above and beyond adornment. They use rings threaded through chains, amulets and birthstones to ward off the ordure of Hollywood, as does Johnny Depp.

Fashion has played a part in the pendant's popularity with the relatively recent vogue for low-cut T-shirts that give neck jewelry a sexier frame than an open-necked shirt. As a rule, the more rough-and-ready the clothes, the sexier and more masculine a gem-set pendant tends to look. Azagury-Partridge has sold her black or white pavé-diamond-set disco ball pendants to guys, while Webster's debut men's jewelry collection, 'Rayman', featured a black rhodium-plated silver cross pendant set with black sapphires and tsavorites. Worn looped through the buttonhole of a lapel, these jeweled charms are a modern interpretation of the fob-watch chain.

Although it may sound obvious, an ostensibly feminine motif in jewelry is alchemically transformed by dark materials such as black sapphires, onyx, spinels and diamonds. Webster's Fly by Night black-diamond butterfly pendant hangs like a bat out of hell, whereas in white diamonds the piece might be a mite too pretty for some men. Boucheron's Cypris Swan pendant, described in 157 round black sapphires, fifteen

round diamonds, rubies and blackened white gold, hangs with glittering malice from a white-gold chain. Similarly, Fennell's limited-edition (fifty-piece) animal pendant charms pavé-set in black and white diamonds, such as the Badger and the Black Cat, are cool rather than cute, as is Webster's Topkat black-diamond fishbone pendant set in white gold.

Van Cleef & Arpels' four-leaf-clover good-luck charm, Alhambra, is one of the sweetest, simplest and most recognizable pieces of twentieth-century fine jewelry. First created in 1968, Alhambra has sustained its status as one of the house's most popular designs. Although the clover motifs are usually scattered symmetrically along chains and pendants, the single malachite clover set in 18ct yellow gold is a handsome talisman for a man, as is the onyx and yellow-gold Vintage Alhambra pendant, or the pendant set with blood-red carnelian. Peretti's portfolio for Tiffany & Co. is similarly distinctive to the house. Three pendant designs in particular speak to men with a minimalist taste: a sterling silver mesh chain suspending a black-jade Open Heart motif, a black ruthenium-over-copper Full Heart pendant on a black silk cord, and Bean, carved out of green jade and set on an 18ct yellow-gold chain.

Men have eyed Peretti's Diamonds by the Yard chains since she created the revolutionary design after joining Tiffany & Co. in 1974. The premise is simple: a needle-thin platinum chain interspersed with open-set round brilliant-cut diamonds at regular or irregular intervals, to be worn singly, casually and in multiples. Peretti said of the design: 'If diamonds are mounted like this the light is different. They look like drops of light, like a stream: very modern.' The night-or-day blasé design that reflected jet-set New York in the 1970s is precisely the style of radically chic white-diamond jewelry that men in tees and jeans can wear with credibility. Those without the conviction for Diamonds by the Yard could begin cautiously with a Chaumet Frisson platinum pendant set with five brilliant-cut diamonds. Leane's 18ct white-gold and diamond thorn heart pendant is another piece that benefits from being worn on its own.

Contemporary jewelers appear to have reached a consensus that a pendant setting for a large stone is most successful with an included, misty emerald as in Azagury-Partridge's Villain pendant (see page 83),

Above. The Riviera necklace by Ara Vartanian. A 22.37ct pentagonal-cut emerald and two trillion-cut diamonds are suspended from a chain of black and white diamonds.

Opposite. A Theo Fennell 18ct white-gold Cross pendant set with 5.8ct of sapphires and 1.17ct of white diamonds.

Above, left. An 18ct yellow-gold bee pendant by Wright & Teague.

Above, right. The Shaun Leane Anvil pendant in yellow-gold vermeil.

Opposite. A portrait by Giovanni Boldini of the artist Lawrence Alexander Harrison in 1902, wearing a sliver of yellow-gold watch chain with a turquoise charm.

which surrounds a cabochon emerald with blackened 18ct yellow-gold bones. Vartanian's 18ct yellow-and-white-gold Riviera necklace frames a 22.37ct emerald with black and white diamonds (see page 224). His emerald is so striking that only a skilled tastemaker would really countenance it. But precedents are already set in the fashion industry for gem-set showpiece necklaces originally made for ladies. Marc Jacobs is often photographed wearing an Andrew Grima yellow-gold and diamond pendant framing a large blue-green dioptase (a coppery mineral) with an open-necked shirt. Giambattista Valli attended the *Punk: Chaos to Couture* Met Gala in New York in 2013 wearing a Bulgari Serpenti white-diamond necklace that coiled twice around the Italian couturier's neck. Both pieces challenge perceptions of what can and can't be worn by men: the inference being that it all depends on the man.

From a piece of utilitarian jewelry worn by men of all classes to a rarefied taste reserved for horologists and dandies, the precious-metal fob-watch chain was a multitasking treasure. An oil of the statesman Lord George Cavendish Bentinck by Samuel Lane (*c.*1836; in the National Portrait Gallery) captures him in his pomp as a celebrated racehorse owner and man of fashion. He wears what appears to be a slim gold chain like a necklace disappearing beneath his collar, which sits wide across the breast of his tailcoat. Two further chains fall into his pocket, which might hold a fob, a seal, an eyeglass, a key or a pencil (invented in 1795). These chatelaine-style chains could be elaborate. In 2016 Lucas Rarities acquired a Victorian chain with two purely decorative ropes ending in domed tassels set with seed pearls and cabochon sapphires.

King Edward VII was photographed as Prince of Wales in 1860, the year before his father's death, wearing the shorter coat that he would popularize; a substantial double chain is visible across his waistcoat, and what appears to be a seal hangs from the pocket. Leaping forward to 1902, Giovanni Boldini painted the bearded artist Lawrence Alexander Harrison in a grey three-piece suit, proudly displaying a sinuous yellow-gold watch chain with what appears to be a decorative turquoise bead hanging casually from the waistcoat. After the First World War, the wristwatch, as championed by another Prince of Wales (the future Duke of Windsor), sent the fob watch into terminal decline. It took Johnny Depp at the *Charles James: Beyond Fashion* Met Gala in New York in 2005 to wear swags of gold watch chain with white tie and make it relevant again.

It was a fashion for ladies to convert watch chains into charm bracelets – one followed by the author's grandmother Hilda Sherwood. On inheriting the rose-gold box chain, the author returned the piece to its original purpose, retaining the charms. But many survived intact and obsolete, making gold watch chains relatively common at auction, and undervalued. Bonhams San Francisco sold a collection of four 10ct and 14ct green-, yellow- and rose-gold chains in 2012 for $1,187, and the auction house's Oxford sales average £500 for lots of two or more yellow-gold Victorian 'Albert' chains with and without fob seals attached.

The fob watch and decorative chain – in sterling silver as well as yellow gold – have made a startling comeback of late among bearded Brooklyn and Shoreditch hipsters and form a nostalgic addition on waistcoats worn with T-shirts to show off full sleeve tattoos, heavy silver chain-link ID bracelets and knuckleduster rings. The hipsters don't care about the protocols of wearing the fob watch in the top jacket pocket or across the waistcoat, and quite right too. As Aldis Hodge proved at the Oscars in 2017 (see page 216), and Dolce & Gabbana proposed for Autumn/Winter 2016–17 at Milan Men's Fashion Week, the multi-chain festoon is an elegant embellishment that directly echoes the way Indian maharajas wore pearls and diamond collet necklaces pinned to the breast.

The plain solid-gold or sterling silver chain necklace is perhaps the most obviously masculine piece of men's jewelry, considering the associations with bikes, cars and industrial machinery. Plain thick chains also resonate with some gay men for their Tom of Finland S&M biker vibe. David Yurman's extra-large box-chain necklace in sterling silver is a classic of its kind, while Bulgari's Monete 18ct yellow-gold link necklaces set with antique bronze coins take the biker chain into the realms of ancient Rome. Fennell has one of the largest collections of belcher-, franco- and chevron-link chains in yellow, white and rose gold and varying girths, including an 18ct rose-gold chain set with eight brilliant-cut diamonds. The more intricate and refined the link, the further one can go towards a pendant rather than a necklace that sits on the collarbone.

Above. Solange Azagury-Partridge's 18ct blackened yellow-gold Bareknuckle pendant.

Opposite. The Stephen Webster 18ct yellow-gold Thames Link bracelet worn as a lapel chain. Tailoring by Henry Poole & Co.

GRIMA

'Very often people want to acquire a piece by Grima for the risk he's taken; his refusal to regard gem stones as inferior to the great jewels, the diamonds, emeralds, sapphires, shows a man in love with his own palette, not just his patron's purse.'

Alexander Walker, foreword to *Grima* (1991)

The jewelry marque Grima is sacred in the closed world of makers, clients and collectors of twentieth-century artist jewelry. From the early 1960s until his death in 2007, Andrew Grima went, creatively, where none of his forebears or contemporaries dared to go. Referring to Grima's most intense period of creativity, in the 1960s and 1970s, his most trusted goldsmith, Tom Scott, called him 'a one-man design movement'. His work is spoken of in the same breath as the sculptors Henry Moore and Barbara Hepworth, rather than jewel houses such as Chaumet and Tiffany & Co. Grima admitted to disliking 'virtually all jewelry that was popular at the time', so he found a new language in jewelry design that had no precedent and has had no equal since.

Preferring textured yellow gold to platinum or silver 'polished like a mirror', Grima used precious stones such as diamonds and emerald crystals as irregular pin spots on designs where the gold took precedence. The Pencil Shaving brooch of 1968 (see page 233) – an elegant curl of textured 18ct yellow gold dotted with brilliant-cut diamonds – is a perfect example of his ingenuity with gold and his sparing use of stones. Mysterious, opaque and irregular materials such as opals, coral, quartz and baroque pearls pleased his eye more than polished stones, and his creativity

soared when he was presented with a dioptase crystal, a slice of agate, a South Sea shell or a shard of pink tourmaline. Led by his materials, Grima's jewels were one-offs and designs were rarely repeated, making his work extremely collectible.

It was not widely known outside the jewelry industry how closely Grima worked with his second wife, Jojo Maughan-Brown, whom he married in 1977, and their daughter Francesca. Jojo Grima is a skilled jeweler with an impressive pedigree. Her great-grandfather Sir Thomas Cullinan discovered and named the largest diamond mine in South Africa, which yielded the largest gem-quality diamond ever mined. The two largest Cullinan stones are set in the British Crown Jewels. Her work, such as a textured yellow-gold and pavé-diamond Twig brooch made in 2013 (see page 234), has a strength and verve similar to Andrew's work and that appeal to men.

Francesca Grima became first in the line of succession in 1998, when the family was living and working in Gstaad, having first quit London for Switzerland in 1986. She spent a decade working at her father's side, learning his language of jewelry design and making her own judgments based on that knowledge and inspiration. In 1991, aged eleven, Francesca was named as 'the new designer rising in the firmament' in the catalogue for the

Above. Andrew Grima 18ct yellow-gold triangle cufflinks, set with carved jadeite (1971).

Opposite. The fashion designer Marc Jacobs wears a dioptase crystal pendant by Grima (1972), set with yellow-gold smooth and textured squares with eight square-cut-diamond accents.

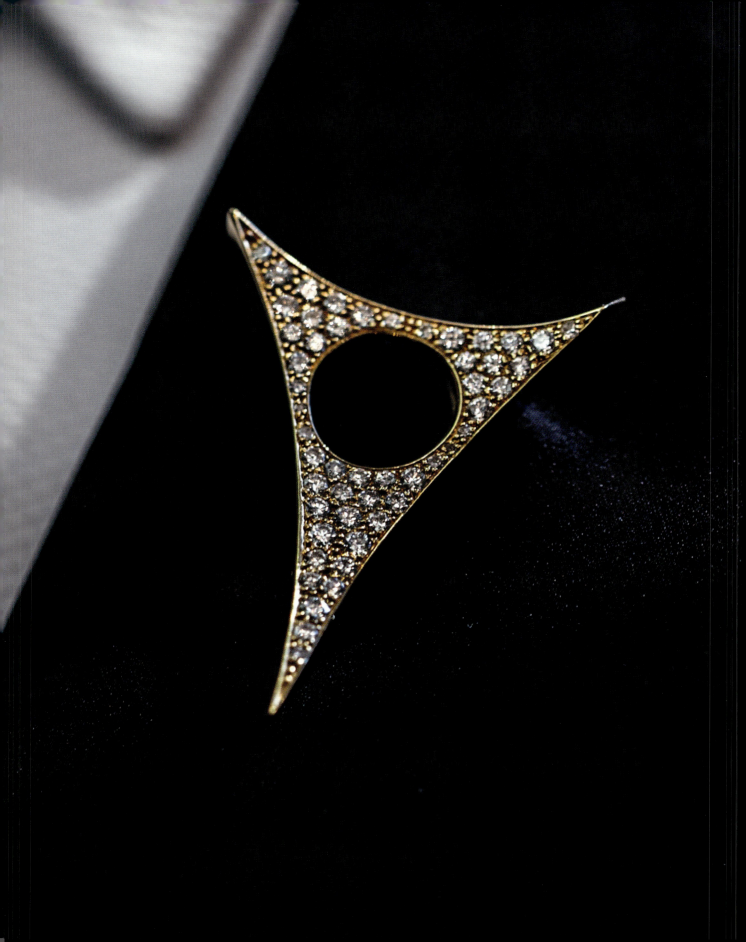

Goldsmiths' Hall 70th birthday retrospective exhibition of Andrew Grima's work. It was Francesca playing with a drinking straw that inspired her father to cast it as a ridged gold brooch set with diamond terminals in 1992.

Now based in London, the Grima studio, directed by Jojo and Francesca, produces an average of thirty new designs per year, made by Scott in the Soho workshop he has inhabited since 1968. The designs echo those of Andrew Grima but are not copies of originals. Some pieces are made for stock and others are commissions. In 2014 Francesca also registered her own trademark for a jewelry collection that owes nothing to her father's back catalogue, and she is enjoying success with younger clients who probably know of no other Grima.

'There are many things I learned from my father that have come into my own designs,' says Francesca. 'The finish; the fact that a piece must be as beautiful from the back as from the front; precision; irregularity in some cases. But then again, my things are quite different.' Of the Grima jewels, Jojo says, 'the work today is ours. They are in a similar vein but not copies. I designed a pair of cufflinks – a delicate Cubist formation of diamonds and sapphires set in white gold – inspired by Andrew's setting for a pair of black-opal ear clips in 1966. The cufflinks are mirror images of each other rather than being identical, as is usual.'

Andrew Grima's style lent itself to men's jewelry, not least because of its unapologetic strength of character and rejection of daintiness or overly pretty designs, and Francesca's work has a similar gutsiness. Andrew's most famous designs for men were sketched at the invitation of the Omega watch company in 1969. Christened 'About Time', Grima's eighty-piece collection comprised sixty watches and matching jewels such as cufflinks, rings and earrings. The watches are audacious futurist designs, with every clock face submerged beneath a gemstone. The designs are so architectural and 'out there' that one hesitates to describe them as watches. They are high-jewelry bracelets that tell the time.

A rectangular, smoky quartz-faced Grima Omega watch framed with bevelled yellow gold and made with a crocodile strap that locks rather than buckles is one of ten made since 1969. Miuccia Prada owns one and Marc Jacobs another. 'The design is so distinctive,' says Jojo, 'and is also the most classical of the Omega collection, so we are in the process of adapting it and having the watch remade as a limited edition.'

Andrew Grima's extraordinary talent continues to energize and inspire the jewels that still bear his family name, and rightly so. His designs have won an unprecedented twelve De Beers Diamond International Awards. In 1966 his engraved yellow-gold and carved ruby brooch won

Above. A Grima 18ct textured yellow-gold Pencil Shaving brooch (1968) scattered with brilliant-cut diamonds. The brooch sold at Bonhams in 2017 for £17,500.

Opposite. A sculptural yellow-gold brooch by Andrew Grima (1969), set with brilliant-cut diamonds.

'There are many things I learned from my father that have come into my own designs. The finish; the fact that a piece must be as beautiful from the back as from the front; precision; irregularity in some cases. But then again, my things are quite different.'
Francesca Grima

'Pieces are now displayed in the Victoria and Albert Museum and are highly collectible, though rare to auction because their owners are reluctant to part with them.'

the Duke of Edinburgh's Award for Elegant Design (now the Prince Philip Designers Prize). The Duke subsequently bought the jewel for the Queen, who gave Andrew Grima her Royal Warrant. Grima also opened outposts in Tokyo, New York and Sydney, as well as an outstanding shop in Zurich with an audacious facade made of the rusting iron plates from the hull of a ship. All the shops were sold in advance of the move to Lugano in 1986; the Goldsmiths' Hall exhibition catalogue of 1991 simply reads: 'credit restrictions and banking crashes suddenly took their toll.'

The Grima marque became a private partnership between Andrew, Jojo and, eventually, Francesca, and clients would travel to Switzerland for solo appointments.

The exile from London explains why the name Grima is perhaps not as familiar as it should be outside connoisseur circles. Pieces are now displayed in the Victoria and Albert Museum and are highly collectible, though rare to auction because their owners are reluctant to part with them. A knockout pentagonal pendant-watch with radiant engraving and a peridot 'glass' watch face suspended from an 18ct yellow-gold kite-link chain sold at Bonhams in 2014 for £20,000, and an 18ct yellow-gold cuff encrusted with carved emeralds and cabochon sapphires (1973) sold at Bonhams in 2016 for £23,750.

www.grimajewellery.com

Left. A Jojo Grima textured yellow-gold and diamond Twig brooch (2013). Tailoring by Turnbull & Asser.

Opposite. A yellow-gold and brilliant-cut-diamond stylized Bark brooch by Andrew Grima (1968). Tailoring by Turnbull & Asser.

HEMMERLE

'What our clients want is to be surprised. For that, we must constantly come up with new ideas. We never produce the same piece twice.'

The story of the Munich-born fourth-generation jeweler Hemmerle is one of Damascene conversion. In 1995 Stefan Hemmerle and his wife, Sylveli, met a client who, in her own words, 'detested flashy gems'. The lady collected and wore early nineteenth-century Prussian Berlin ironwork jewelry: the base metal filigree ornamentation exchanged for gold to help the Napoleonic war effort. Following the lady's brief, Hemmerle set an important white diamond into a simple, minimal ring of textured iron. According to company lore, 'Stefan decided the time was right to break with the past and transform the jewel into a true contemporary work of art.'

In successive years, Stefan and Sylveli, their son Christian and their daughter-in-law Yasmin have established the house as a maker of artist jewelry of unparalleled originality. Rare and exotic wood, aluminium, steel, copper, river pebbles and camouflage beadwork are given equal precedence with precious stones; red gold is preferable to the gleam of 18ct yellow gold, and brown, green, orange and canary diamonds tend to outnumber white. The setting is the story. As Christian says, 'there are no ordinary materials, only the beauty of nature.' Of the conventional settings of rubies, sapphires and emeralds with white diamonds, he says: 'They are tied to value. Our aim is to excite and surprise with our experimentation in materials and to push existing conventions and boundaries.'

Although Hemmerle's Bauhaus-inspired minimalist settings dominated the house's work in the 1990s, the aesthetic evolved into fiendishly complex naturalistic brooches that have as much resonance with male collectors as with female. One of the most desirable 'project' collections was 'Delicious Jewels' (2011), designed by Christian and Yasmin. This bravura suite of brooches included the three-dimensional Artichoke described in copper, white gold and silver with a heart of purple sapphires, and Pea, with demantoid garnet leaves and jade beads replicating the peas in the pod. From 'Nature's Jewels' (2014), outstanding brooches included a split copper and diamond Pomegranate revealing rubellite bead seeds, and a heavenly Physalis with crisp gold leaves surrounding the melo-pearl fruit. The masterpiece is the Corn brooch from 'Delicious Jewels', an ear rendered in copper, gold, silver and diamonds that is split open to reveal rows of oriental pearls.

'The juxtaposition of materials we use gives our jewelry a different edge,' says Christian of the average of 230 pieces the house creates each year in its workshop in the flagship in Maximilianstrasse, Munich, that has been its home since 1904. By auction standards, Hemmerle has entered the major league on the secondary market with unseemly haste. In 2016 a Hemmerle diamond-and-copper ring sold at Christie's New York for $162,500. In the same year

Clockwise from top left.
Hemmerle brooches from the 'Delicious Jewels' collection of 2011: red-sapphire Radish, oriental pearl Sweet Corn, jade Pea and diamond Cauliflower.

Sotheby's Geneva sold a 12.03ct octagonal step-cut sapphire ring for $299,009, and in 2010 Hemmerle's copper-and-spinel Harmony bangle lined with white gold was acquired by the Victoria and Albert Museum for its William and Judith Bollinger Gallery. In 2014 an Egyptian-inspired Harmony bangle in exotic wood set with turquoise and tsavorite garnets entered the permanent collection of the Cooper Hewitt, Smithsonian Design Museum.

Hemmerle is an example to heritage jewel houses of how to draw a line under the past, however prestigious. The company was founded in 1893 by the brothers Joseph and Anton Hemmerle to specialize in medals and orders for the Bavarian royal family and other nobility. They had missed the glory years of King Ludwig II's reign, which ended in the monarch's suicide or murder in 1886, but served the subsequent Prince Regent Luitpold and King Ludwig III. Hemmerle won a prize at the Paris Exposition in 1900 for its gold, enamel and amethyst *Jugendstil* (art nouveau) Bishop's Cross. The line drawn by Stefan and Sylveli Hemmerle occurred only two years after the house's centenary, for which Stefan had designed a gold Bavarian lion embedded with a colour drift of more than 2,000 diamonds and sapphires.

'Our jewelry is unique,' says Christian Hemmerle. 'A lot of people admire it and some don't appreciate it at all. There are definitely some people in this world who say "Why would I want to wear un-precious material?" A hundred years ago it was forbidden in France to mix gold with un-precious materials, so our product would have been forbidden.' Hemmerle's approach to setting – both pragmatic and contradictory – creates tension between the precious and base that gives the pieces a masculine sensibility. Only Hemmerle could take an exceptional cabochon sapphire and place it on a trelliswork of iron to create a brutally

The Hemmerle Evergreen Oak brooch in copper, brass, gold, silver and diamonds.

beautiful brooch or lapel pin. 'To my mind, there's something sculptural about jewelry,' says Christian. 'The third dimension must be shown to advantage.'

Hemmerle's cufflinks are a study in simplicity. The signature link, a pyramid of metal set with a chain and bar, is rendered in red gold, iron and bronze. Round white-gold and silver links are set with misty cabochon sapphires with a 1960s futurist feel. It is not for nothing that Christian has said, 'What they [clients] come for is a beautiful piece of German engineering.' Combining copper, gold, diamonds and mammoth ivory in one piece of jewelry requires not only a fearless imagination but also a fifteen-strong workshop to rise to the challenge. Stefan said, 'it was not my intention to shock, though I did want to inspire.'

When Hemmerle shows at the annual Masterpiece fair in Chelsea, London – a world-class art, antiques and jewelry showcase – one never knows whether vintage cameos, Roman micro-mosaic setting or old cut diamonds will be part of the palette. Stefan, who once set a significant Kashmir sapphire with river pebbles, says that 'copying can never be art. Art is inspiration not imitation.' Hemmerle's 'combination of realism with whimsy' – as the late collector and jewelry writer John Traina described it – can easily take more than 200 hours per piece to realize. This places Hemmerle jewelry on a high plane both creatively and financially. According to Harry Winston's former world president Patricia Hambrecht, 'Stefan and Sylveli are among the few jewelers working today who elevate their craft to a true level of artistry.'

www.hemmerle.com

WRIGHT & TEAGUE

'As artists and jewelers, we know it matters to our clients
and collectors that our jewels come from our hands: literally.'

Husband and wife artist jewelers Gary Wright and Sheila Teague have forged a discerning international clientele with precious metalwork that references techniques of the ancient Greeks, Romans and Egyptians. Married with a minimal, sculptural sensibility, it produces timeless design. The shapes they sculpt on the benches in their studio in Shoreditch, east London, reach back to civilizations in which jewelry for affluent men was the rule rather than the exception. Their angled, ridged and textured 18ct yellow-gold Zambezi ring with its highly polished interior could grace the finger of an African chieftain, while the yellow-gold Naga serpent ring that coils sinuously around the finger could sit in the Cairo Museum as one of the treasures excavated from Tutankhamun's tomb in 1922 (see page 33).

Coming from the minds and hands of a man and a woman, Wright & Teague's work is almost impossible to classify as jewelry for ladies or gentlemen. It would be advantageous for a straight couple to share the pleasure of a single piece of jewelry, such as the Mystic necklace or bracelet (see page 189) made up of combinations of handmade beads in silver, yellow gold and rose gold with thumbprints pressed into the metal. Wright & Teague's Iliad cuff, an 8-millimetre (1/3-inch) curved concave bracelet of textured 18ct yellow gold, is another deeply satisfying 'timeshare' piece of jewelry. Perhaps the

very sparing use of gemstones adds to the house's appeal for men.

Wright and Teague's journey towards their unique handwriting began when the couple met at Central Saint Martins College of Art & Design in London. They shared the belief that 'jewelry doesn't just adorn the body, it intrigues the mind,' but worked independently for the first decade after graduating. Wright made figurative artist jewelry inspired by Salvador Dalí and René Magritte, while Teague produced sculptural, Bauhaus-inspired pieces from aluminium, rejecting precious metal and gemstones completely. 'I always made men's jewelry,' she says. 'It was the 1970s, which was a flamboyant, avant-garde era for men's fashion. It was Bowie, men in brooches, make-up. It frightened some people but it excited us.'

Wright and Teague (who married in 1977) united creatively from 1983, when they were invited to make costume jewelry for the BBC's eight-part drama *The Cleopatras*. Although the epic wasn't as intended a worthy successor to *I Claudius*, the costumes were spectacular. The pair crafted thousands of collars, crowns, cuffs, rings and earrings for principals and extras, working largely in brass inlaid in bronzed leather. 'We used a considerable amount of car paint spray,' says Wright. 'The jewelry was inspired by ancient Egypt, but it was our artists' impression, so there was license to create,' says Teague. Having

Wright & Teague's 18ct yellow-gold In Dreams inscription ring, inspired by the Roy Orbison lyric 'In dreams I walk with you.'

Above. Wright & Teague's trio of Enyo irregular rings in textured 18ct yellow gold, 18ct rose gold and platinum.

Opposite. The Wright & Teague 18ct granulated yellow-gold Hi Tex ring.

enjoyed working intensively on the project, the two decided to work in tandem, beginning with pieces made in brass and copper. The early television work would lead to a prestigious commission for the Cate Blanchett films *Elizabeth* (1998) and *Elizabeth: The Golden Age* (2007).

In the 1980s Wright & Teague rode the wave of the resurgence in great British fashion. They produced biannual themed jewelry collections with extra accessories such as scarves and gloves, and worked with designers such as Katharine Hamnett, Wendy Dagworthy, Paul Smith and Joseph. They showed at fashion weeks in London and Paris and sold to Japan, Italy and America. In the early 1990s Patrick Demarchelier shot their jewelry as styled by Grace Coddington in *Vogue*. 'Then we got to a stage when we just didn't want to tear everything up every six months and start again,' says Teague.

The Wright & Teague style we recognize today – characterized by tactile, organic shapes, talismanic symbols, textured goldwork and a curious ability to look ancient and relentlessly modern at the same time – was finally given an appropriate showcase in Dover Street in 2008. 'People laughed their heads off when we said we were opening in Mayfair,' says Teague. 'It was so uncool to be in Mayfair next to all those trophy jewelers who make pieces that show your

neighbour that you've got more money than they have. We were selling art worn as jewelry, not mainstream bling.'

The shop became known as a lord of men's rings, such as the thick, irregular 18ct yellow-gold Daedalus ring and the pleasing 'curved coin' Pegasus ring. Wright & Teague are democratic, making the same shape – such as the textured, irregular circle of the Enyo ring – in silver as well as yellow gold, white gold and platinum. A Daedalus in silver retails for £200, compared to £5,500 for the same piece in platinum. It was a smart move to make entry-level pieces in silver for a younger customer as an introduction to the house: 'We love to work with gold, but we'd like our jewelry to be for everybody who enjoys it.'

In 2012 Wright & Teague was invited to open a shop in the Burlington Arcade, off Piccadilly. This treasure chest of a space seemed to be a more appropriate showcase for the work, with workshops in the cellars that run the length and breadth of the arcade. During the Burlington Arcade years Wright & Teague executed three showpiece commissions: the Pleiades looped-gold Lunula collar for the exhibition 'Gold: Power and Allure' (2012) at Goldsmiths' Hall, a gold-and-ruby ring and earrings for a Gemfields showcase (2013) with the company's brand ambassador Mila Kunis, and a set of 18ct gold gaiters

Left. The 18ct yellow-gold 'dancing dots' Capella ring by Wright & Teague.

and armbands modelled in Carine Roitfeld's 'Ultimate Gold Collection' fashion show for the AIDS organization amfAR at the Hôtel du Cap-Eden-Roc in Antibes in 2013.

Today, Wright & Teague has relocated its showrooms and workshops to Spitalfields in the East End of London, and clients visit by appointment. 'We don't want to go down the purely bespoke route,' says Wright, 'and we have had what we called our gap year after leaving the Burlington Arcade shop. We're doing a showcase in LA this year, and that might be the right approach for now.' Of all the jewelers in *Jewelry for Gentlemen*, Wright & Teague

is perhaps the least divisive, which is their compliment. Even men who don't traditionally wear jewelry are won over by the house's purity of design and integrity of handcraft. Examine the evidence: a solid 18ct yellow-gold Bee cufflink that Wright cast from 'life', with expertly detailed fretwork wings; a pink-gold Byzantine Orthodox cross pendant suspended from a heavy curb-link chain; or a sterling silver man's ring with 'Forget me Not' inscribed in Roman text.

www.wrightandteague.com

Opposite. The sterling silver and 18ct yellow-gold Iliad cuff, sterling silver and 18ct yellow-gold Pegasus ring and 18ct yellow-gold Stud ring, all by Wright & Teague.

Left. Wright & Teague's 18ct yellow-gold Bee cufflinks.

BIBLIOGRAPHY

Aga Khan, Princess Catherine, and Pierre Rainero. *Jeweled Splendours of the Art Deco Era: The Prince and Princess Sadruddin Aga Khan Collection*. London: Thames & Hudson, 2017

Becker, Vivienne. *Art Nouveau Jewelry*. London: Thames & Hudson, 1998

Bennett, David, and Daniela Mascetti. *Understanding Jewellery*. Woodbridge: Antique Collectors' Club, 1989

Chadour-Sampson, Beatriz, and Hubert Bari. *Pearls*. London: V&A Publishing, 2013

Corbett, Patricia. *Verdura: The Life and Work of a Master Jeweler*. London: Thames & Hudson, 2002

——. *Jewelry by Suzanne Belperron: My Style is my Signature*. London: Thames & Hudson, 2016

Etherington-Smith, Meredith. *Graff: The Most Fabulous Jewels in the World*. London: Cultureshock Media, 2007

Geoffrey-Schnetter, Bérénice, and Vivienne Becker. *Cartier Panthère: Legends*. Paris: Assouline, 2015

Gere, Charlotte, and John Culme. *Garrard: The Crown Jewellers for 150 Years*. London: Quartet, 1993

Gregorietti, Guido. *Jewellery Through the Ages*. London: Paul Hamlyn, 1969

Grima, Andrew. *Grima*. Düsseldorf: Johann Willsberger, 1991

Hue-Williams, Sarah. *Hidden Gems: Stories from the Saleroom*. London: Unicorn Press, 2016

Irvine-Bray, Elizabeth. *Paul Flato: Jeweler to the Stars*. London: Antique Collectors' Club, 2010

Loring, John. *Tiffany Diamonds*. New York: Abrams, 2005

——. *Tiffany Coloured Gems*. New York: Abrams, 2007

McCarthy, Kiaran. *Fabergé in London*. London: ACC Art Books, 2016

Mascetti, Daniela, and Amanda Triossi. *Bulgari*. Milan: Leonardo, 1996

Menkes, Suzy. *The Windsor Style*. London: Grafton Books, 1987

Meylan, Vincent. *Van Cleef & Arpels: Treasures and Legends*. London: Antique Collectors' Club, 2014

Munn, Geoffrey. *Wartski: The First Hundred and Fifty Years*. London: Antique Collectors' Club, 2015

Neret, Gilles. *Boucheron: Four Generations of a World-Renowned Jeweler*. New York: Rizzoli, 1988

Papi, Stefano. *The Jewels of the Romanovs: Family and Court*. London: Thames & Hudson, 2010

Phillips, Clare (ed.). *Bejewelled by Tiffany: 1837–1987*. New Haven and London: Yale University Press, 2006

Possémé, Evelyne (ed.). *Van Cleef & Arpels: The Art of High Jewellery*. Paris: Les Arts Décoratifs, 2012

Proddow, Penny, Debra Healy and Marion Fasel. *Hollywood Jewels: Movies, Jewelry, Stars*. New York: Abrams, 1992

——, and Marion Fasel. *Diamonds: A Century of Spectacular Jewels*. New York: Abrams, 1996

Rudoe, Judy. *Cartier: 1900–1939*. London: British Museum Press, 1997

Sassoon, Adrian. *Jewels by JAR*. New York: Yale University Press, 2013

Solodkoff, Alexander von. *The Jewel Album of Tsar Nicholas II*. London: Ermitage, 1997

Stronge, Susan. *Bejewelled: Treasures of the Al Thani Collection*. London: V&A Publishing, 2015

Tait, Hugh (ed.). *7,000 Years of Jewellery*. London: British Museum Press, 2006

Woolton, Carol. *Floral Jewels: From the World's Leading Designers*. London: Prestel, 2014

——. *Vogue: The Jewellery*. London: Octopus Books, 2015

Young-Sanchez, Margaret. *Cartier in the 20th Century*. Paris. Vendôme Press, 2014

Zucker, Benjamin. *Gems and Jewels: A Connoisseur's Guide*. London: Thames & Hudson, 1984

GLOSSARY

aigrette Feathered, jeweled hair or turban ornament.

amethyst Purple quartz semi-precious stone characterized by its fragility and believed by the ancient Romans to guard against drunkenness.

aquamarine In its purest form, a perfect sea-blue gemstone.

baguette cut Rectangular, step-cut diamond traditionally used for eternity rings.

bezel Upper part of a finger ring, holding a gemstone in place.

bloodstone Dark-green **chalcedony** with red spots and veins.

brilliant cut Diamond cut with triangular and kite-shaped facets radiating from a central point.

briolette cut Teardrop-shaped gemstone cut with small, triangular facets.

cabochon cut Precious or semi-precious stone polished into a smooth dome without being cut into facets.

cameo Hardstone or gem into which a design is cut in relief.

carat Unit of weight for gemstones.

chalcedony Translucent quartz found worldwide; also a blanket term for **cabochon** hardstones and bead varieties such as agate, **bloodstone**, carnelian, chrysoprase, jasper, **onyx**, sardonyx and tiger's eye.

citrine Yellow to golden quartz mineral. Known as the 'success stone' in the language of gemstones.

coral Carved from the skeletal material of sea branch coral, a hard, opaque red-to-pink organic substance used in jewelry.

cushion cut Square or rectangular gemstone with rounded corners.

emerald Green precious gemstone originally mined in Colombia and noted for its fragility and **inclusions**.

enamel Coloured glass or vitreous glaze fused on to a metallic surface, a technique perfected by Fabergé in the late nineteenth century and known as guilloché.

engraving Technique of cutting patterns into a surface with a sharp tool; also known as intaglio. When intended as a seal, the device is executed in reverse.

fancy Coloured diamonds.

filigree A decorative pattern of open setting made of precious-metal wires, sometimes soldered to a background.

garnet Red gemstone used in jewelry since the Middle Ages and most popular **cabochon** cut in men's cufflinks. Demantoid garnets, discovered in the Ural Mountains in 1851, are green and known as Ural emeralds for their rich colour dispersion.

girdle Narrow band separating the crown and pavilion of a cut gemstone.

haematite Grey iron ore with a lustre, used in jewelry since Egyptian times and mined in Cumbria, northern England.

inclusions Naturally occurring imperfections that hamper a gemstone's clarity; now appreciated by contemporary jewelers as signs of character in coloured stones.

jade Common name for two similar fine-grained minerals: jadeite and nephrite. Multicoloured, but prized most highly in the deep-green-to-white register.

lapis lazuli Blue hardstone streaked with gold, highly prized by the ancient Egyptian pharaohs. Originally mined in Afghanistan, but since found in Argentina, Chile, the United States and Russia.

malachite Found in Zaire, a green-banded mineral that was particularly popular in nineteenth-century Russian imperial jewelry and objets d'art.

marquise cut Long, narrow oval stone with pointed ends.

moonstone Translucent gem with a soft blue-white sheen called adularescence; found in Myanmar and Sri Lanka.

old European cut Term used for a diamond cut before the acceptance of the American **brilliant cut**.

onyx Opaque black **chalcedony**.

opal A **cabochon**-cut stone with a fiery play of rainbow colours, originally mined in Slovakia but since discovered in Australia. Black opals were discovered in Australia in 1902. Fire opals were found in Mexico and are characterized by their semi-transparency.

parure Matching set of jewelry, such as a dress set and ring.

pavé Small gemstones set closely together to pave a continuous surface of precious metal.

pear cut Teardrop-shaped diamond cut combining the rounded bottom of a brilliant cut and the tapered point of a marquise cut.

pearl Natural pearls are hard, smooth or bevelled beads created by salt and freshwater molluscs and are now extremely rare. Cultured pearls are farmed.

peridot Olive or yellowish-green gemstone mined since antiquity and popularized in men's jewelry in late nineteenth-century Europe.

precious stones The major arcana of the gemstone family: diamonds, rubies, emeralds and sapphires.

PVD (physical vapour disposition) Technique of blasting metal with another metal, such as black steel with black titanium, to obtain a stronger metal plating.

quartz Transparent or semi-transparent crystals, the most abundant mineral on the Earth's surface. Used faceted in men's rings, quartz magnifies underlying materials such as **coral** or **opal**.

rose cut Round stone with triangular facets in a dome shape over a flat base; one of the oldest diamond cuts.

ruby Red gemstone that exceeds only the most unusual pink, blue and green diamonds in rarity. Pure Burmese rubies that have not been oiled or irradiated to enhance the colour are the most highly prized.

sapphire Precious gemstone, most highly prized when mined in Kashmir. Blue sapphires are arguably the most popular precious stones for men's jewelry.

spinel Red gemstone often mistaken for a ruby, as in the case of the Black Prince's ruby set in the band of HM The Queen's Imperial State Crown.

star sapphire Natural phenomenon in **cabochon-cut sapphires** and **rubies**, known as an asterism, whereby the reflection of light creates the illusion of a star-like figure in **inclusions**.

table cut Largest facet on the top of a cut gemstone. An early style of gem-cutting based on the octahedron.

tanzanite Blue gemstone discovered in Tanzania in 1966, named by Tiffany & Co. and distinguishable from a **sapphire** by its purple-blue hue.

topaz Stone in tones of yellow, gold and brown, fragile and infinitely rarer than the citrines that are often mistaken for it. Imperial topaz mined in Brazil is reddish-orange and the most highly prized.

torc Metal collar or neck ring made in the Bronze and Iron ages in Europe for tribal leaders.

tourmaline Heavily flawed but highly collectible chameleon stone that typically comes in two colours that trick the eye.

trapeze cut Four-sided diamond cut with two parallel sides. Traditionally a step cut, but can now be faceted as a **brilliant cut**.

triangular cut (also known as trilliant and trillion) A diamond cut from a flat rough that makes it appear larger than its **carat** weight indicates.

tsavorite Bright-green gemstone discovered in Kenya in 1968 and introduced by Tiffany & Co.; still found only in Kenya and Tanzania.

turquoise Hard, opaque, pale-blue stone, one of the first gemstones used in jewelry. For 3,000 years Iran was the major source, but turquoise is now found in Arizona and New Mexico. Jewelry set with it is highly collectible since the mines are now all but extinct.

vermeil Silver coated with gold; a contemporary term for silver gilt.

DIRECTORY

ASPREY (1781)

On the same premises at 167 New Bond Street since 1847, Asprey sells what is traditionally known as fancy goods, such as silver and silver-gilt dinner services, dressing cases, jewelry, leather trunks and writing cases. It has held the Royal Warrants of every monarch from Queen Victoria to Queen Elizabeth II, although the most extravagant commissions were bespoken by the maharajas of Patiala and Cooch Behar in the 1920s. The firm left family hands in 1995, when it was purchased by Prince Jefri of Brunei. Asprey merged briefly with the Crown Jeweler Garrard in 1998, but they separated again in 2002.
www.asprey.com

BAILEY BANKS & BIDDLE (1832)

Founded in Philadelphia, the silversmith and coin-engraver Bailey Banks & Biddle produced presentation swords for General Ulysses S. Grant, and the funeral medal for Abraham Lincoln. The firm began to produce jewelry in the late nineteenth century; it also designed stationery, as well as striking the Medal of Honor in 1905. Its jewelry produced in the belle époque is the most collectible.
www.baileybanksandbiddle.com

BAPST & FALIZE (1880)

The skilled enamellist, goldsmith and jewelry designer Lucien Falize joined forces with Germain Bapst, descendent of French royal jewelers, in 1880, and the partnership would continue until 1892. Both Falize and Bapst were influenced by Renaissance jewels, and married sixteenth-century design with art nouveau to create treasures such as jeweled, enamelled pendants, Etruscan-style filigree yellow-gold cameo rings and 18ct yellow-gold foliate brooches with naked cherubs holding diamond-set drapery.

SUZANNE BELPERRON (1932)

Suzanne Belperron famously declared *'Mon Style est ma Signature,'* hence not signing any of her work and giving antiques dealers and collectors headaches ever since over attribution. Her first jewelry designs were for the Maison René Boivin in 1919, directed by the founder's widow, Jeanne. From 1924 Belperron and her husband lived in Montmartre, and, although her work for Boivin was uncredited, her modernist jewels were understood to be the soul of the house. In 1932 Belperron left Boivin to become artistic director of Maison Bernard Herz, where her style was liberated from the geometry of art deco. Her jewels were lauded by such fashion leaders as Elsa Schiaparelli, Diana Vreeland, Mona Bismarck and the Duchess of Windsor. After the Second World War Belperron founded a new company with Herz's son Jean. She was awarded the Legion d'Honneur in 1963 and retired in 1975. The firm of Belperron was revived in 2015 under the direction of Nico Landrigan, whose father, Ward, had purchased and relaunched Verdura in 1985.
www.belperron.com

BERLIOZ LEROY (1920)

Monsieur Leroy and Mademoiselle Berlioz's eponymous firm at 19 Rue de la Paix produced high art deco masterpieces such as vanity cases, sautoirs, cuffs and dress clips. An advertisement in French *Vogue* for Berlioz Leroy painted by Jean-Gabriel Domergue in 1922 clearly demonstrates the Orientalist, exotic influence on the house's jewelry. In 1923 *Le Figaro* wrote: 'They create the rarest jewels in Paris, the most artistic.' The house closed in the late 1930s.

BLACK, STARR & FROST (1810)

The oldest jeweler in America was founded at 164 Broadway, New York, by Isaac Marquand and traded under 'the sign of the golden eagle'. Trading as Ball, Black & Co, the company displayed its jewelry at the Great Exhibition in Crystal Palace, London, in 1851, as well as a solid gold tea service. Black, Starr & Frost was incorporated in 1874 and enjoyed a golden age in the belle époque, when America's millionaire dynasties Vanderbilt, Guggenheim, Carnegie and Astor began commissioning American crown jewels from the house. The firm's fortunes fell and it was reduced to a single Californian flagship by 2006. Now owned by the Molina Group, it trades under the slogan 'Bringing back American luxury.'
www.blackstarrfrost.com

RENÉ BOIVIN (1890)

The goldsmith René Boivin began his career producing jewelry for Mellerio and Boucheron, but found a private clientele for his delicate diamond jewelry set in the fashionable garland style. In 1893 he married Jeanne (sister of the celebrated couturier Paul Poiret), who would save the house of Boivin after her husband and her son Pierre died in 1917. Madame Boivin created jewels in her own handwriting with a brilliance and boldness that did for jewelry what her brother Paul had for haute couture. In 1919 she employed the talented Suzanne Belperron, who would design some of the house's most original pieces. Belperron left Boivin in 1932, a year after the company had moved to new premises on the Avenue de l'Opéra, where Madame employed Juliette Moutard as her new designer, alongside her daughter Germaine Boivin. The latter continued to direct the house after her mother's death in 1959, until she too retired in 1976.

BUCCELLATI (1919)

After the First World War, Mario Buccellati returned to Milan and bought the jeweler Beltrami & Besnati, for which he had worked. Trading from a shop on Largo Santa Margherita, Buccellati cemented his success when he exhibited his work in Madrid and won the patronage of the Spanish royal family. By 1925 he had boutiques in Rome (on the Via Condotti) and Florence. Buccellati jewelry is distinguished by filigree gold and platinum work that emulates techniques of lacemaking. The jewels drape around the body with the lightness and fluidity of satin or chiffon. The firm opened in New York, on 51st Street, in 1951, and within a decade had opened on Fifth Avenue and in Palm Beach. In 1979 it was the first Italian jeweler to open a flagship on the Place Vendôme in Paris. Today, Mario Buccellati's great-granddaughter Lucrezia is the creative director of the house.
www.buccellati.com

BULGARI (1884)

Founded by the Greek silversmith Sotirios Voulgaris, Bulgari opened on the Via Sistina in Rome and would become synonymous with the *Dolce Vita* style. It originally sold antique silver and jewelry, and even after Voulgaris opened premises on the Via dei Condotti, in 1894, he still referred to his business as the Old Curiosity Shop. His sons Constantino and Giorgio inherited the business in 1932 and began to make jewelry influenced by the French masters. Avid collectors of Bulgari included Elizabeth Taylor, Sophia Loren, Claudia Cardinale and Gina Lollobrigida. The brand became a global powerhouse, including perfume, watches and a collection of luxury hotels, under its CEO until 2011, Francesco Trapani (Giorgio's grandson), and his uncles Paolo and Nicola. In 2011 the world's largest luxury-goods group, LVMH, bought out the Bulgari family's shares for $5.2 billion, and in 2017 Bulgari launched its first men's jewelry collection.
www.bulgari.com

CASTELLANI (1814)

The art dealer, master goldsmith and jeweler Fortunato Pio Castellani traded from the ground floor of the Palazzo Raggi on the Via del Corso, Rome. He was ideally placed to witness the boom in archaeological excavations, and was inspired to make reproductions of Etruscan and Roman gold jewelry. With the benevolence of his patron the Duke of Sermoneta and the assistance of his sons Alessandro and Augusto, Castellani perfected the ancient art of granulating gold, and by the 1850s produced only archaeological revival jewelry. The Duke of Sermoneta encouraged Castellani to explore the use of mosaic in his jewelry and ever more elaborate enamelwork. In 1859 Alessandro Castellani's political views gave him the choice of imprisonment or exile from Rome; he chose the latter and opened a shop on the Champs-Élysées. In 1881 Castellani moved to the Piazza Fontana di Trevi in Rome and was directed by Augusto and his son Alfredo. The business continued until Alfredo's death in 1930.

CHAUMET (1780)

Founded by father and son Marie-Etienne and François-Regnault Nitot, Nitot & Fils was the Court Jeweller to Emperor Napoleon I and was (and is) famed for setting tiaras such as those in the grand parures made for the empresses Joséphine and Marie-Louise. After the fall of Napoleon, the house led fashion in jewelry with naturalistic settings of white diamonds that would bloom fully at the court of Emperor Napoleon III and Eugénie. The company was christened Chaumet in 1889, when Joseph Chaumet took over the company from his father-in-law, Prosper Morel. Joseph Chaumet came to be recognized as an undisputed master of the belle époque, and later set magnificent jewels, such as two pear-cut diamonds into a collar for the Maharaja of Indore in 1911.

www.chaumet.com

MARILYN COOPERMAN (1963)

The Canadian-born artist jeweler Marilyn Cooperman worked as a fashion writer and illustrator in New Zealand before moving to New York in 1963 to design her own line. She worked from a studio in the jeweler Fred Leighton's Greenwich Village

boutique, and sold at Saks, Bergdorf Goodman and Bloomingdale's. She was made editor-in-chief of *Vogue Patterns*, before Leighton asked her to work with him redesigning and re-setting antique jewelry. She launched her own company in 1994 with a showcase in Los Angeles. Cooperman works by appointment from her New York studio, and is acknowledged in the same breath as JAR and Gimel for her glorious brooches that paint with gemstones.

www.marilyncooperman.com

FABERGÉ (1842)

The House of Fabergé was founded in St Petersburg in 1842 by the master goldsmith Gustav Fabergé, but it was his son Peter Carl Fabergé (1846–1920) who elevated the firm to goldsmith by special appointment to the Romanov tsars Alexander III and Nicholas II. Carl trained extensively with leading goldsmiths in Europe before returning to St Petersburg in 1872. The house is most famous for the jeweled imperial Easter Eggs commissioned by the tsars and their tsarinas, of which forty-three are known to survive. Fabergé also made a vast number of cufflinks and stick pins for Nicholas II, and was famed for the guilloché enamel technique that was displayed in jewelry, cigarette cases, clocks and picture frames. At the turn of the twentieth century, at the height of Fabergé's fame, the house had branches in London and Moscow. It was nationalized by the Bolsheviks in 1918. Wrangling over the Fabergé trademark was not resolved until 2013, when the gem mining company Gemfields bought the marque, which had been relaunched as a fine jeweler in 2007.

www.faberge.com

FALIZE (1856)

Lucien Falize joined the workshop of his goldsmith father, Alexis, in 1856, but experienced a creative epiphany in 1862, when he was introduced to Japanese art at the International Exhibition in London. He created cloisonné jewels enamelled in

the Japanese style that would inspire Lalique and Fabergé. In 1871 Falize moved his family firm to the Avenue de l'Opera, and he won both the Grand Prix and a Legion d'Honneur for work shown at the Exposition Universelle in 1878. In 1880 he went into partnership with the German jeweler Germain Bapst; Bapst & Falize lasted until 1892 and produced a glorious collection of neo-Renaissance jewels. After Falize's death in 1897, the firm was directed by his sons, trading as Falize Frères. The business died with the eldest, André, in 1936.

PAUL FLATO (1923)

Born into an affluent cattle-ranching family in Texas, Flato moved to Manhattan to attend Columbia University but dropped out after his parents cut off his allowance. In 1923, after serving an apprenticeship with a jeweler on Fifth Avenue, he opened his own shop, at East 57th Street and Fifth Avenue. He clearly appreciated exceptional design, employing Fulco di Verdura and David Webb. His friendship with the diamond dealer Harry Winston resulted in such show-stopping pieces as the necklace set with the 125.65ct Jonker diamond. Flato was a socialite and wit, and infused his jewelry with surrealist humour: a Gold Digger bracelet set with a gold pickaxe and a diamond-and-ruby bracelet inspired by Mae West's corset. When he opened a shop on Sunset Boulevard in Beverly Hills in 1938, his clients included Marlene Dietrich, Greta Garbo, Rita Hayworth, Elsa Schiaparelli, Anita Loos, Fanny Brice, Paulette Goddard, Katharine Hepburn and Joan Crawford. Sadly, he tried to ease cash-flow problems by pawning jewels belonging to dealers and clients, and he was imprisoned for grand larceny in 1943. He died in relative obscurity in 1999.

GARRARD (1735)

A royal jeweler since 1735, the House of Garrard was appointed Crown Jeweller by Queen Victoria in 1843 and held the Royal Warrant until 2007. Garrard is largely responsible for the design of the British

Crown Jewels as they are today. In 1852, at the command of Prince Albert, the house re-cut the Koh-i-Noor diamond. It refashioned St Edward's Crown for the coronation of King Edward VII in 1902, set the largest flawless diamond in the world – Cullinan I – into the Sovereign's Sceptre, and made two entirely new crowns for King George V and Queen Mary in 1911 to wear at the Coronation Durbar in Delhi. In 1953 Garrard re-set the Imperial State Crown for Queen Elizabeth II; it also made Lady Diana Spencer's sapphire engagement ring in 1981, now worn by the Duchess of Cambridge. The present creative director is Stephen Webster.
www.garrard.com

GIULIANO (c.1860)

The Italian Carlo Giuliano opened a workshop on Frith Street, Soho, where he perfected the Renaissance Revival style that pleased Queen Victoria, her daughter the Empress Frederick of Prussia and her daughter-in-law the Princess of Wales. His elaborate Renaissance pendants, carved garnet stick pins and Indian-inspired enamel cufflinks are some of the most collectible pieces of men's jewelry to come to auction. Early Giuliano pieces were sold at London jewelers such as Hancocks and Robert Phillips, until Carlo opened a showroom in Piccadilly in 1874. His sons Carlo and Arthur inherited the business in 1895, and continued it until Arthur's suicide in 1914.

JAR (1977)

The cult of JAR (Joel Arthur Rosenthal), the Harvard-educated American jeweler in Paris, is well served by the fact that he and his partner in both business and life, Pierre Jeannet, see clients by introduction only, make fewer than 100 unique pieces per year, and abstain completely from publicity or promotion. His masterpieces are seen only in the circles of the ladies and gentlemen for whom he agrees to make them, and in the hallowed halls of the

Metropolitan Museum of Art in New York and Somerset House in London. When the actress Ellen Barkin included seventeen pieces by JAR in her jewelry auction at Christie's New York in 2006, estimates quadrupled and the public became aware of JAR's genius. JAR says he has 'pushed pavé work to the absolute limit, eliminating as much metal as possible'. He has perfected a metal made from silver, gold and nickel to a closely guarded formula, and led the way with blackened-gold settings that allow his rich colours to effervesce. In JAR's hands, a natural-pearl necklace made for the Al Thani family echoes Cartier's works for the Indian maharajas in the early twentieth century.

LACLOCHE FRÈRES (1875)

The Spanish brothers Léopold, Jacques, Jules and Fernand LaCloche began a successful business selling fine jewelry. After Jacques died in a train crash, the remaining three brothers opened a shop on the Rue de la Paix in Paris in 1901. By 1908 LaCloche Frères had seven European branches, and the house began to develop the Oriental and Chinese-influenced style that would make it one of the great names in the art deco era. After the Russian Revolution, LaCloche Frères London took over Fabergé's flagship. The jeweled jabot pin so symbolic of jazz age jewelry was perfected by the house, which also became a master in the creation of vanity cases, cigarette cases, compacts and lipstick holders encrusted with jeweled Egyptian motifs. The Wall Street Crash in 1929 closed all its premises but a showroom on the Rue de la Paix and the shop in the Carlton hotel on the Boulevard de la Croisette, Cannes. Throughout the 1930s LaCloche Frères excelled in the design of dress clips and brooches, including a design inspired by curled wood shavings that anticipated Grima in the 1970s. The Paris shop closed in 1966.
www.laclochefreres.com

RENÉ LALIQUE (1885)

René Lalique, 'the father of modern jewelry', trained at the bench of Louis Aucoc while attending classes at the École des Arts Décoratifs, before studying in England. He sold pieces to Cartier and Boucheron before developing pieces influenced by the popular Japonism. Lalique, who opened his first shop in 1887, rejected the prevailing garland style in diamond jewelry in favour of more exotic materials such as mother-of-pearl, ivory, horn, enamel, glass and wood. His delicate, naturalistic art nouveau designs won him the Legion d'Honneur after the Paris Exposition Universelle of 1900. Fashion leaders such as Sarah Bernhard and Marchesa Luisa Casati collected Lalique, while his sensuous nude goddesses and figurative beauties were worn as cufflinks and stick pins by the beaux of the belle époque. From 1907 his interest turned to glassmaking, beginning with perfume bottles for François Coty and reaching a pinnacle with the interiors of the Côte d'Azur Pullman express train, the luxury liner *Normandie* and Madame Vionnet's couture salon. Lalique died in 1945, long after jewelry production had ceased at the house. In 2012 the house produced its first high jewelry collection – 'L'Odyssée du Feu Sacré' – in almost a century.
www.lalique.com

PIERRE STERLÉ (1934)

Born into a family of civil servants, Pierre Sterlé was introduced to jewelry design when his father was reported missing, presumed dead, in 1915 while serving in the Great War. He was sent to live in Paris with his uncle Maynier-Pincon, who became his jewelry master. Sterlé opened his own workshop in 1934 and supplied designs for Boucheron and Chaumet before designing a collection under his own name in 1939 that was championed by Colette, the queen of literary Paris. In 1943 he moved to an upper floor on the Avenue de l'Opéra, and in the early 1950s he was known as the 'couturier of jewelry' by such couturiers as Jacques Fath, Christian Dior, Cristóbal Balenciaga and Jean Dessès. Sterlé won the De Beers Diamond Award three times between 1953 and 1955, and became famed for his cocktail jewelry. His gold work was revolutionary: twisting, knotting, plaiting and creating *fil d'ange* (angel wire) knitted like chainmail. But opening a boutique (in 1969) proved fatal to his business. In 1976 Sterlé liquidated his company and became a design consultant for Chaumet; he died in 1978.

DAVID WEBB (1948)
David Webb's 'quintessential American jewelry' captured the post-Second World War ebullience of Manhattan with bold, colourful designs often inspired by costume jewelry but made with precious stones. Born in North Carolina, Webb was repairing jewelry in Greenwich Village by the age of seventeen and, thanks to his southern charm, good looks and unique talent, opened his first shop at twenty-three. He was backed by the socialite Antoinette Quilleret, and the family of his co-founder and business manager, Nina Silberstein, continues to run David Webb today. Webb was influenced by Fabergé's enamelwork and the geometric pizzazz of art deco. His work appealed particularly to such strong women as Diana Vreeland, Jackie Onassis, Ava Gardner, Elizabeth Taylor and Princess Grace of Monaco. Webb died tragically young from pancreatic cancer in 1975. For men, he was a maestro of cufflink design, crafting bejeweled, enamelled animal-head links as well as more severe pieces, such as twisted gold hoops and the hammered 18ct yellow-gold-and-diamond nail designs from his 'Toolbox' collection.
www.davidwebb.com

JULES & LOUIS WIESE (1845)
Jules Wiese worked on a small canvas, creating neo-Renaissance brooches, rings and pendants in distressed yellow gold dominated by human and mythological creatures and intricately set stones in the antique style. He was born in Berlin in 1818 and was apprenticed to the Prussian court jeweler before moving in 1939 to Paris, where he became workshop manager for the house of Froment-Meurice. He registered his own hallmark in 1844 and showed at the Paris Exposition, where he won a First Class. In 1880 his son Louis took over the workshop; he remained faithful to the neo-Renaissance style developed by his father, as well as re-creating pieces to his father's designs. Although less well-known than his contemporary Castellani, Louis Wiese was an acknowledged master goldsmith and formed men's cufflinks, stick pins and rings from neo-Gothic grotesques and gargoyles as well as snakes, antique coins and heraldic motifs. The house closed its doors in 1923, by which time art deco jewelry had rendered Renaissance Revival jewels unfashionable and obsolete. Today Wiese brooches, cufflinks and stick pins are highly collectible for men.

HARRY WINSTON (1932)
The son of Ukrainian immigrants to New York, showman Harry Winston worked in his father's shop and was fabled, aged twelve, to have recognized a 2ct emerald in a pawn shop, bought it for 25 cents then sold it days later for $800. Winston was both a skilled self-taught gemmologist and an entrepreneur with a fox's instinct for the kill. In the 1920s he formed the Premier Diamond Company, buying estate jewelry, re-setting it and doubling his money. In 1935 Winston bought the Jonker rough diamond, which weighed 726ct. The largest stone to come from it, the 149.90ct D-flawless Jonker I, was sold to King Farouk of Egypt in 1949. Winston was the first jeweler to loan diamonds to actresses for the Academy Award ceremonies, beginning in 1944, and he bought and kept as many famous diamonds as he sold to Elizabeth Taylor, Jackie Onassis and the Duchess of Windsor. He bought Evalyn Walsh McLean's blue Hope Diamond in 1949 and treasured it until he donated it to the Smithsonian in 1958. In 1952 it was reported in *Life* magazine that he owned 'the second largest collection of historic jewels after the British royal family'. In 1960 Winston moved to 718 Fifth Avenue, where the firm still trades. Of all the fine jewelers, he was the first to invest heavily in gentlemen's watch design. The firm's collaboration in 2007 on a platinum and white-diamond men's collection by the fashion designer Thom Browne was pioneering. Today Winston's men's jewelry collection is led by cufflinks and dress studs made from the zirconium-based alloy Zalium, white gold and solitaire white diamonds.
www.harrywinston.com

JAMES SHERWOOD
www.james-sherwood.com
www.jewelleryforgentlemen.com

BIOGRAPHIES

HH SHEIKH HAMAD BIN ABDULLAH AL THANI is a member of the Qatari Royal Family and cousin to the Emir. He is the founder of The Al Thani Collection Foundation, which is best known for its exceptional holding of Indian and Indian-inspired gems and jewelry. Sheikh Hamad graduated with honours in Political Science and International Relations from the University of Coventry in 2002 and is Chief Executive of his family's private investment company, QIPCO.

JAMES SHERWOOD has worked in luxury publishing for many years, first as a contributor to the *Independent on Sunday*, *Financial Times*, *The Telegraph*, *The Times* and *The International Herald Tribune* and then as founding editor-at-large of *The Rake*. Specializing in tailoring and fine jewelry, his books for Thames & Hudson include *Savile Row* (2010, 2017), *Fashion at Royal Ascot* (2011), *The Perfect Gentleman* (2012) and *James Sherwood's Discriminating Guide to London* (2015).

ACKNOWLEDGMENTS

The author would like to thank all the exceptionally talented jewelers profiled in *Jewelry for Gentlemen*, who were generous to a fault with their enthusiasm and knowledge. This is my fifth book working with my publisher Lucas Dietrich at Thames & Hudson, and he has proved a patient and trusted friend. It is also my fifth book working with Peter Dawson at Grade Design, who is quite simply the best. Principal photographer Andy Barnham worked like a Trojan and makes the fiendishly difficult art of photographing gemstones look effortless. There wouldn't be a book without Fleur Jones at Thames & Hudson. Having written about fine jewelry for more than two decades now – with a sabbatical on Savile Row – it was truly remarkable to have such a welcome back from the ladies and gentlemen who work in a business I have always loved. Those in the following roll call went far above the call of duty to make *Jewelry for Gentlemen* as visually rich as I hope you'll agree it is. It was very important for me to photograph the jewels in the context of how smart men in the twenty-first century dress. Huge thanks to Simon Cundey and Anthony Rowland at Henry Poole & Co, Jema Avedian, Dean Gomilsek-Cole and Shaun Gordon at Turnbull & Asser, and the talented Sir Tom Baker. Cartier's Silvia Steffen-Ehl and Harriet Mathias introduced me to Cartier's creative director of image, style and heritage, Pierre Rainero, and the Al Thani collection on show in Paris. Cartier's London archivist Jenny Rourke kindly allowed me to mine her knowledge. Gillian McVey opened the door to David Yurman and an inspiring meeting with Evan Yurman in New York. Joan Rolls arranged for me to photograph Van Cleef & Arpels masterpieces in London, and Emma Beckett introduced me to Ara Vartanian and the Boucheron archive collection. The antique jewelers in London – Amy and Guy Burton at Hancocks, Geoffrey Munn and Thomas Holman at Wartski, Mark Evans and Omar Vaja at Bentley & Skinner, Cartier and Verdura connoisseur Harry Fane, and Sam Loxton and Francesca Martin-Gutierrez at Lucas Rarities – loaned masterpieces for me to photograph. Thank you to Tiffany & Co. Archivist Annamarie Sandecki and Assistant Archivist Cristina Vignone for eleventh-hour assistance from New York. It is always a pleasure to work with Gary Wright and Sheila Teague (Wright & Teague) and with Jojo and Francesca Grima. Bonhams director of jewelry, Europe, Jean Ghika, was generous with images from previous auctions, and Bonhams global CEO, Matthew Girling, encouraged me in the early stages of the project. Sotheby's senior director and head of press office, Mitzi Mina, answered every request for images and organized tea with Sotheby's worldwide chairman, international jewelry division, David Bennett.

INDEX

Page numbers in *italics* refer to captions

PICTURE CREDITS

On the cover (top to bottom): Tiffany & Co. pin (see page 168); Van Cleef & Arpels brooch (see page 152); diamond Skull and Snake ring by Theo Fennell; Panthère de Cartier ring (see page 34).

A charming Victorian enamel and old-cut diamond pheasant lapel pin sold at Bonhams.